Managing Human Resources and Collective Bargaining

DANIEL R. TOMAL
AND CRAIG A. SCHILLING

ROWMAN & LITTLEFIELD EDUCATION
A Division of
ROWMAN & LITTLEFIELD PUBLISHERS, INC.
Lanham • New York • Toronto • Plymouth, UK

Published by Rowman & Littlefield Education
A division of Rowman & Littlefield Publishers, Inc.
A wholly owned subsidary of The Rowman & Littlefield Publishing Group, Inc.
4501 Forbes Boulevard, Suite 200, Lanham, Maryland 20706
www.rowman.com

10 Thornbury Road, Plymouth PL6 7PP, United Kingdom

British Library Cataloguing in Publication Information Available

Library of Congress Cataloging-in-Publication Data

Tomal, Daniel R.
  Managing human resources and collective bargaining / Daniel R. Tomal and Craig A. Schilling.
     pages cm
  Includes bibliographical references and index.
  ISBN 978-1-4758-0263-4 (cloth : alk. paper) — ISBN 978-1-4758-0264-1 (pbk. : alk. paper) — ISBN 978-1-4758-0265-8 (electronic) 1. School personnel management—United States. 2. School management and organization—United States. 3. Collective bargaining—Education—United States. 4. Collective bargaining—Teachers—United States. I. Schilling, Craig A., 1950- II. Title.
  LB2831.58.T66 2013
  371.2'01—dc23
                                                                         2012050562

∞™ The paper used in this publication meets the minimum requirements of American National Standard for Information Sciences—Permanence of Paper for Printed Library Materials, ANSI/NISO Z39.48-1992.

Printed in the United States of America

Contents

Rebore: #1 Organiz'l Dimensions
2. HR Planning
3. Recruitment
4. Selection
5. Placem & Induction
6. staff dvpt.
7. Perf Eval
8. Compensation.
9. Collective Negotiations
10. Legal, Ethical

Rebore #2,
#3-sel

VGN

Eval

1,2 3-5 6-8

10 Legal Ethics

Foreword

For many, many years, the role of school administration and business management, regardless of its plethora of other titles, has been perceived as one primarily dealing with accounting and finance. This can be demonstrated by reviewing the job descriptions and the available published literature of the 1960s and 1970s. Unfortunately, the profession of school business management contributed to this misperception. Over the past thirty years, the growth in the number of tasks and functions assigned and performed by the school business manager has been significant. Not only this growth in responsibilities but also the growing understanding of the relationship between the use of resources and student achievement has brought the position of school business manager into the spotlight.

The need and opportunities for the incumbent and the new career seeker in school business management for professional development has not always kept pace with that of "what and how" the school business manager is expected to perform at a high level. This is true at the university level and at the association level and in the United States and abroad. Degree programs specific to school business management and state certification requirements have been narrow and/or nonexistent. In the past, the few universities that did offer graduate degrees in school business management basically provided a master's degree in educational administration (the usual principalship course offering), an additional finance and accounting course, and in some instances a facility course. In this day and age, this is clearly inadequate for what society needs as far as trained school business managers go.

Scholarly field-based research in the total domain of school business management that could serve as the basis for a knowledge base reflected through a body of literature has been lacking. Over the past several decades, publications that treat in a comprehensive fashion all elements of school business management have started to appear.

This work by Professors Tomal and Schilling is a welcome addition to the literature relating to school administration and business management. What makes this text such a valuable addition to our literature? First, both Dr. Tomal and Dr. Schilling are scholar-practitioners. Both have followed career paths that many would find hard to duplicate. Both have served in the profession with distinction, worked in the trenches, and thereby gained an experience base that is clearly reflected in their work. Both have served their profession in leadership positions at the local, state, national, and international levels and made significant contributions at each level.

Second, the overall organization of each chapter has been thoughtfully laid out. All chapters have been written in a consistent format, and the sequence of content has been consistent in scope and relevancy.

Third, the book has been written in a practical approach, offering strategies that are straightforward and easy to apply. All the numerous principles and strategies have been developed from a research/theoretical base and then accompanied by a comprehensive summary of chapter topics, case studies, exercises, and discussion questions that are well thought out, clearly defined, and thought provoking. The material is not "busy work" for the students who are serious about their study of school human resources or for incumbent school leaders seeking to improve their own performance and enhance their value to their employer.

Fourth, the reference section that follows each chapter provides a rich starting point for the reader who wants to take a deeper journey into the chapter topic. The references also demonstrate that the authors are current and familiar with the field.

Fifth, each chapter begins with a set of objectives that are cross-referenced to standards of ISLLC (Interstate School Leaders Licensure Consortium) and ELCC (Educational Leadership Constituent Council). The content of each chapter then supports the objectives in a clear and succinct manner.

Sixth, this is a book that can serve well those who work at all levels of education such as universities and public, private, and charter school systems. While reference and appendixes reflect heavily on the standards, laws, and practices in the United States, this book has utility beyond the U.S. borders, and in fact they can be a source of reflection and impact on any school in positive ways. What may not be required in one setting may still have use as a voluntary paradigm in another.

I congratulate Drs. Tomal and Schilling on this sterling accomplishment. This is a good read for those serious about school improvement and increasing the effectiveness and efficiency of any school or schools. It is a welcome addition to our literature. It will serve as a great tool for those who are shaping the minds of the next generation of school business managers.

R. E. Everett, Ph.D., former professor of school business management, Northern Illinois University, and former executive director, Illinois Association of School Business Officials

Preface

Human resource management is one of the most critical responsibilities of school administrators. This book has been written based upon years of study, research, and consulting in school administration. The strategies described in this book have been found successful in operating at both the school district and school building levels and are especially centered on providing information on connecting human resource management and student achievement. While primarily directed toward public schools, the strategies in this book can also be effective for private elementary and secondary schools and charter schools. The information and strategies are practical and useful techniques that can be used by any school administrator or graduate human resource and collective bargaining student who desires to optimize human resources.

The first chapter provides practical strategies for human resources planning. Extensive examples are provided in developing strategic plans, succession planning, and how to plan successors for incumbent positions. Last, a comprehensive description of federal Equal Employment Opportunity Commission (EEOC) laws and executive orders are given with practical examples of how they impact human resource management.

Chapter 2 covers recruiting and selecting applicants. Topics include methods of recruiting, selecting the best candidates, and laws and policies. Several examples and sample forms are also included in this chapter.

The next chapter includes the topics of mentoring new employees. Also, professional development and establishing and conducting performance appraisal systems are included. Practical examples and forms are provided in this chapter. A challenging and realistic case study is included at the end of the chapter to test comprehension of the material.

Chapter 4 covers leading and motivating employees. Relevant topics of principles of leadership, leading, and motivating employees are covered. Several popular leadership theories such as situational leadership, the X and Y model, the leadership grid, expectancy model, two-factor motivational theory, the equity motivation model, team leadership, and total quality management are presented as they relate to school leadership.

The topic of building collaboration and disciplining employees are covered in chapter 5. Other areas include managing conflict and terminating employees. Several practical examples and forms are also provided, and the chapter concludes with a comprehensive case study.

Chapter 6 includes the topic of benefits and compensation. Several areas include establishing benefits and compensation programs, salary structures, and types of compensation programs. Several exhibits and examples of compensation programs are provided.

The seventh chapter covers the topic of unions and collective bargaining. This chapter also includes the history of unions, negotiation strategies, and the collective bargaining process. There are also case situations and practical examples of collective bargaining throughout the chapter. There is a challenging concluding case study that can be helpful in understanding and applying the principles and strategies of the chapter.

The last chapter includes the area of managing human resources, conducting audits, creating efficiencies, position control, and technology. Several process mapping and technology checklists are included. Several illustrations and a comprehensive case study are included at the end of the chapter.

At the end of the book, there are several helpful resources. Some of these include employee rights, employer and union rights and obligations, a summary of major laws, laws enforced by the EEOC, prohibited employment policies, and practices of the EEOC. These reference materials can be very useful in understanding governmental policies, laws, and executive orders regulating human resources.

FEATURES OF THE BOOK

Nothing can be worse than reading a book that is boring, dry, and impractical for educators. This book is unique in that it provides many engaging examples that can be used by all educators. One feature of the book is the correlation of the objectives of each chapter with professional organizational standards of the National Council for Accreditation of Teacher Education (NCATE), the Specialized Professional Association (SPA) of the Educational Leadership Constituent Council (ELCC), the Interstate School Leaders Licensure Consortium (ISLLC), and National Standards for Quality Online Teaching (from the International Association for K–12 Online Learning, iNACOL) and Southern Regional Education Board (SREB).

Another valuable feature of the book is the incorporation of many diverse strategies related to school leadership; motivation; recruiting and selecting candidates; and disciplining, compensating and bargaining with, and terminating employees. They are provided in a straightforward and practical manner. The topics in this book are useful for any administrator who desires to optimize fiscal, facility, and human resources.

Other features of this book include:

- Practical examples of human resource management,
- Examples of basic school compensation structures,
- Strategies for leading and motivating employees in the school environment,
- Models of leadership and motivational theories that have been proven in the business world as applied to the educational setting,
- A comprehensive description of conducting strategic and succession planning,
- Up-to-date guidelines, EEOC laws, and legal considerations,
- Practical strategies in giving employees feedback and taking action for improvement,
- Examples of discipline offenses and how to administer disciplinary action,
- A review of some of the major federal and state laws and guidelines,
- Strategies in managing conflict and how to promote teamwork and collaboration, and
- Strategies in collective bargaining.

Last, this book also contains a rich source of educational and reference materials so that educators can apply the concepts for school resource management. Some of these materials include:

- Case illustrations and figures in applying leadership and human resource strategies,
- Examples of motivation strategies that can improve academic performance,
- A sample of field-based educational issues, and
- Actual examples of assessments and real-life case studies.

ORGANIZATION OF THE BOOK

The organization of this book has been written in a straightforward manner so educators can understand the critical school resource management. Each chapter builds upon the others. However, each chapter is also distinct in itself because it covers specific topics that relate to the three topics. Last, each chapter includes basic theories and examples of applying these theories, case studies, and exercises and discussion.

Acknowledgments

Appreciation is extended to the many people who have assisted and worked with the authors. Special appreciation is given to the authors' students, colleagues, and former business associates in the corporate world: Susan Webb for typing part of the manuscript; and Laurel Schilling for her editorial review and suggestions. The authors would also like to recognize and extend appreciation to the many school districts where the authors have provided consulting, such as the Chicago Public Schools, Bellwood School District 88, Cicero School District 99, Lake Central School Corporation, Proviso Township High Schools, West Chicago District 33, School District 131, Michigan City Township High Schools, Findlay Schools, Glenbrook High School District 225, West Northfield District 31, Lindop School District 92, Schiller Park District 81, Norridge School District 80, Rich Township High School District 227, Marquardt School District 15, Concordia University Chicago, and Lutheran Church Missouri Synod schools. Last, the authors would like to extend gratitude to the many people who endorsed this book and provided insight for this project.

1

Human Resources Planning

OBJECTIVES

At the conclusion of this chapter, you will be able to:

1. Understand the human resources planning process (ELCC 3.3; ISLLC 1, 3).
2. Define the steps of strategic and succession planning (ELCC 3.3; ISLLC 1, 3).
3. Understand critical team values necessary to collaboratively develop a vision and effectively manage human resources (ELCC 1.1, 1.2, 1.3, 5.1, 5.2, 5.3; ISLLC 1, 2, 3, 5).
4. Define critical laws and executive orders of the Equal Employment Opportunity Commission (ELCC 6.1, 6.2, 6.3; ISLLC 3, 6).
5. Describe how Equal Employment Opportunity Commission laws and regulations impact human resources planning (ELCC 6.1, 6.2, 6.3; ISLLC 3, 6).

STRATEGIC PLANNING

One of the most important resources of any organization is the employees. While there are many facets to managing human resources, the foundation begins with proper planning. There is an old adage that states, "Those who fail to plan, plan to fail." Planning in human resources involves assessing organizational needs, predicting the future, establishing and communicating operational goals, conducting job analyses, and identifying key positions needed by the organization (Marler, 2009).

Human resources planning ensures that an organization has the correct number of people in the right places at the right time who have the necessary skills and performance to complete the institution's objectives. An organization cannot accomplish any goals without qualified people. Proper planning allows administrators to ensure successful transitions and ensure that people can accomplish the tasks needed of an organization in a smooth and harmonious manner. While some school districts approach human resources planning differently, all administrators need to be involved in human resources forecasting to ensure that there are capable people performing the necessary tasks of the organization (Earley, Weindling, Bubb, & Glenn, 2009).

Strategic planning is one of the most popular strategies utilized by educators to prepare a comprehensive plan for meeting workforce needs for the future (Thompson, 2010). Essentially, strategic planning involves answering the questions of "What is our situation today?" "Where do we want to go?" "How can we best get there?" and "Who are the people who are going to champion the strategies in getting us there?"

Strategic planning is a technique that originated in corporate America and has become a popular tool in education. This process allows administrators to identify critical issues that need to be addressed, establish an overall vision, develop critical goals and key strategies to accomplish the vision, establish metrics to measure performance, and plan resources.

Some of the benefits of strategic planning include:

1. Builds upon collaboration and the expertise of people,
2. Allows for creativity in addressing major issues,
3. Stimulates visionary thinking to improve an organization,
4. Provides empowerment for people to accomplish goals,
5. Improves the performance of the organization, and
6. Helps in predicting financial budgets for a school district.

While strategic planning has many benefits, it needs to be undertaken in a structured manner. If managed poorly, the costs of strategic planning can exceed the benefits. Individuals may waste valuable time in brainstorming ideas that are unproductive if the process is not facilitated well. Some limitations include:

1. People may concentrate on the most immediate needs without regard for long-term needs, *short : long-term needs*
2. Administrators may fail in successfully implementing strategies,
3. Poor accountability,
4. Lack of resources, and
5. Lack of follow-up to the strategic initiatives. *Monitoring*

Therefore, when strategic planning is undertaken, proper resources are needed to ensure success. Some of these include providing sufficient time to develop the strategic plan, allowing for creativity, selecting proper people who will participate and develop the plan, and providing sufficient financial resources to implement the strategic plan.

The procedure for conducting strategic planning can vary from organization to organization. Typically, strategic planning should begin at the top level and then be facilitated throughout the entire organization. For example, strategic planning may start at the district level, conducted at the school building level, and then at the department level. In this way all organizational units are supporting the top district-level initiatives. However, strategic planning can be independently conducted at the school building level as long as the people understand the established goals of the district.

Steps to Conducting Strategic Planning
1. Assemble the Team. Select the members of the strategic planning team.
2. Determine Resources and Logistics. Agree on the logistics and resources needed for completing the strategic plan.
3. Determine Format. Agree on the final format and components of the strategic plan.
4. Write Values Statement. Discuss critical values and behaviors and formulate a values statement for the organization.
5. Write a Vision Statement. Write a vision statement and, if necessary, a mission statement.
6. Complete a SWOT (Strengths, Weaknesses, Opportunities, and Threats) Analysis. Complete a detailed SWOT analysis.

SWOT AUTOPSY

GOALS
↓
STRATEGIES — Measurables / perf indicators

7. Write Major Goals. Write major goals for the strategic plan based upon the SWOT items.
8. Prioritize Major Goals. Prioritize the major goals and determine time-frames (one, three, or five years).
9. Write Key Strategies. Develop key strategies for each of the major goals.
10. Include Metrics. Include metrics (measurable score cards or performance indicators) for each strategic goal and financial estimates for funding key strategies.
11. Assign Champions. Assign champions to major goals to be accountable for them.
12. Write Strategic Plan. Write the strategic plan and gain approval.
13. Integrate the Strategic Plan into the Performance Management System. The goals and people who are accountable should be included into the goals setting and appraisal process.
14. Conduct Awareness Sessions. Inform people of the strategic plan for their roles. Get people involved into the process and implementing the strategic plan.
15. Monitor and Assess Progress. Establish a system of monitoring the progress of the strategic plan and documenting results.
16. Conduct Reviews of Individuals' Performance. Conduct individual mid-year and year-end reviews of people and the goals. Provide rewards and incentives.
17. Evaluate the Strategic Planning Process. Evaluate what went well and not so well with the strategic planning process and improve the process for next time.

The process of conducting strategic planning involves several critical steps (see "Steps to Conducting Strategic Planning"). The first step is to assemble the strategic planning team. Typically, this team will consist of the top administrator (e.g., superintendent or principal) and his or her administrators and selected teachers and staff members. This team will not only be responsible for developing the final product but will also be critical in driving the process and determining the resources that are needed for completing the strategic plan, step 2. Typically this team will meet to plan all the resources needed and decide whether an outside facilitator will be used for the process.

The use of an outside facilitator can be helpful in allowing the entire team to concentrate on the content of the plan rather than needing to facilitate and record all the information, which can be done by the facilitator. The facilitator can also conduct the process, reduce pressure from superiors, and help keep the group on track. While there may be costs in utilizing an outside facilitator, this person can be valuable in providing input regarding his or her experience in conducting strategic planning with other organizations as well as helping the team when they encounter difficult interpersonal and process issues.

The strategic plan is a road map for the organization and should include specific human resource initiatives that support the educational goals of the district. The strategic plan should also be a comprehensive document that supports all the units of the entire organization, such as building facilities, human resources, equipment and supplies, engineering, technology, financial and budgeting resources, and educational programs and materials. The school improvement plan (SIP) is similar to strategic planning, but it generally centers on student learning, such as curriculum and instruction, student and faculty programs, and student behavior that impacts the school. Therefore the strategic plan is the overall road map that includes all these facets in operating a school district or school.

The third step necessitates the team agreeing upon an acceptable format for the strategic plan document. There are many variations in the components comprised in a strategic plan. For example, some schools may not have both a vision and mission statement. Also depending upon the complexity of a school district, the number of departmental or unit plans can vary. "Components of a Strategic Plan" shows an example of the typical components of a strategic plan. There may also be a plan for all the essential units of an organization, such as academic departments, engineering department, transportation, safety and security, custodial, and so on.

It is important that the team determine the logistics in completing the strategic plan, such as how often they will meet, location, schedule, and materials and resources. Some teams may schedule multiple sessions that range from two to four hours over an extended period of time, such as six weeks. However other teams may conduct a retreat where they may spend a couple of concentrated days developing the plan. Each team must decide the overall logistics that are best for them and least obtrusive to the operation of the school.

Components of a Strategic Plan
 1. Executive summary
 2. Table of contents
 3. Core competencies
 4. SWOT analysis
 5. Critical success factors
 6. Vision statement (and mission statement)
 7. Major goals
 8. Key strategies and financial needs
 9. Metrics (performance indicators)
10. Department-level goals and strategies
11. Status summary spreadsheet
12. Appendix

Step 4 involves the team constructing a *values statement.* It is important to establish the key values that drive the behavior of people within the organization. Establishing values is a prerequisite to writing a *vision statement.* For example, if the school is a religious-based organization, the values will be different from a public institution. Establishing these values can help in crafting the ultimate vision and mission statements. When examining the values, some of the questions that can help guide the team include "What values are important to us?" "What do we stand for?" "What specific behaviors do we value?" "How do we desire to treat each other?" and "How do we want to be viewed by our stakeholders?" Typically, by answering these questions, a team will arrive at a values statement. In addition, team members can participate in *values exercises* to establish common team values for the group.

"Example of Team Values" shows a list of typical values that team members could review and rank in order of importance for their team's success in working together in a group. For example, in this exercise the team members might determine that a value of individual power can be destructive to the overall cohesiveness of the team. In other words, the team members may decide that seeking individual power should be restrained while other values, such as honesty and trust, should be encouraged and reinforced for achieving team success for the organization.

Example of Team Values

Achievement (achieving/exceeding our school goals)

Altruism (giving of our time, passion, energy, commitment)

Collaboration (teamwork and working well with others)

Creativity (being innovative, offering new ideas, change)

Honesty and Trust (being honest and trustworthy with each other)

Justice (fairness and respect to each other)

Knowledge (continued learning beyond what we already know)

Commitment (total faithfulness to each other and school)

Morality (doing the right thing, having good ethics)

Power (ability to get what you want)

Writing the vision statement, step 5, typically includes thoughtful reflection regarding the desired culture of the organization. Some helpful statements consist of "Striving for the highest quality learning within the school"; "Striving to treat each other fairly through honesty, respect, and open communications"; "Providing an opportunity for everyone to grow professionally"; or "Having a passion for innovation, originality, and continued intellectual growth." Some teams may elect to write a *mission statement* in addition to a vision statement. A vision statement or a mission statement or both can be written. A mission statement tends to be a broad goal, such as "To explore the galaxies." A vision statement is typically much more concrete, such as "To land a man on the moon and watch him walk." While the statements are similar, the vision statement concentrates more on behaviors and is often more concrete and measurable. For example, a school district may have a mission statement "To allow all students to grow to their fullest capacity" versus a vision statement, such as "All students will score in the top 20 percent of the nation on standardized tests." However all organizations are unique organisms and need to determine what kind of vision and mission statements best reflect the desires of the stakeholders.

Step 6 consists of completing the SWOT analysis. SWOT stands for *Strengths, Weaknesses, Opportunities*, and *Threats*. In this step, the team identifies the strengths of the school. Examples include a good core reputation, strong leadership, competent and experienced teachers, and high employee morale and satisfaction. Weaknesses might include lack of technology equipment and competencies, inadequate facilities, poor safety, and inadequate transportation for students. Opportunities are those situations that offer potential additional support to the school district in achieving higher performance levels that include establishing business relationships, utilizing university expertise, writing grants, and increasing financial resources.

Threats are typically situations that might hinder the success of the school district, which could include an aging faculty, high employee attrition, political unrest within the community, and potential high immigrant growth that may require additional programs and resources. Establishing the strengths, weaknesses, opportunities and threats can become the basis from which the strategic plan is developed. Often, the strengths are recognized and sometimes improved, but the weaknesses need to be addressed by establishing concrete *goals* and *key strategies*. In addition, opportunities and threats need to be examined, and strategic goals can be written based upon them.

Step 7 entails writing the *major goals* for the strategic plan. These major goals should be written using SMART criteria. SMART goals consist of being *Specific, Measurable, Attainable, Realistic*, and *Timely*. Once the major goals are written, it is important to carefully examine the goals and prioritize them, step 8. A team may write too many goals that cannot be realistically achieved. The team members should decide which are the highest-priority goals and establish time frames for each of the goals such as one-, three-, or five-year increments.

Prioritizing the major goals and establishing time frames goals, step 8, involves negotiation, collaboration, and resource management. Team members need to be respectful of each other and establish *ground rules* in how they conduct themselves in the meetings. Typical functional behaviors include seeking and giving opinions, elaborating, and encouraging people to praise others and be open to new ideas. Nonfunctional behaviors are being too aggressive, self-confessing, playing politics, pushing self-interest above the group, withdrawal, or clowning around and disrupting the group.

Once the major goals are written, key strategies must be developed, step 9. For example, if someone wants to become a millionaire, the key strategy outlines the process in how to get the money. If a major school goal is to advance the knowledge and technical skills of the faculty, then one key strategy might be to hire a technology consultant and to conduct technology training sessions. Also included within the strategy should be well-written *metrics*, step 10. Metrics, sometimes called *performance indicators*, are the scorecards upon which the level performance is to be established. For example, if the major goal is to improve technological knowledge and the key strategy is to provide training for people, a metric might be to achieve 50 percent competency within three months.

Step 11 requires assigning *champions* to the goals so that people can be held accountable for accomplishing them. Champions act as crusaders in promoting the goals, providing resources needed to accomplish the goals, and measuring the results. Without passionate champions supporting the goals, it is easy to lack the follow-through necessary to achieve them. The champions for the goals may or may not include members of the strategic planning team, and they should periodically meet to review their progress. Champions should be selected based upon the criteria of high credibility and strong desire for achieving results. They also should be people who have good interpersonal skills and who can work collaboratively with people to support their efforts in accomplishing the goals.

Step 12 involves writing the strategic plan, which requires careful review and editing by the members of the team to produce the final document. Outside readers can be obtained to help critique the final document and ensure that it is to acceptable quality and standards and that they are in line with federal and state policies and guidelines. The final strategic plan is often approved by the strategic planning team, superintendent, or school board.

Step 13 consists of integrating a strategic plan into the *performance management system*. This entails selecting the key goals and people and to hold them accountable through the goal-setting and performance-appraisal process. This step is often overlooked in the strategic-planning process. It is important that there is linkage between the goals and individuals' goals so people can be evaluated based upon the results. In some organizations actual bonuses are established and given to individuals who exceed the goals, which provides incentives for meeting and exceeding the goals.

Step 14 involves making everyone aware of the strategic plan. The plan is not going to be accepted or worthwhile if it is locked up in a cabinet and

LINKAGE - CRITICAL - RESULTS

no one knows about it. The strategic plan is a living document that should be integrated within the entire organization, and everyone should become involved in implementing it. Therefore, conducting awareness sessions for everyone within the organization is critical and how they will be involved in achieving them. Also, once the strategic plan is done, then a copy should be given to the departmental chairs so that they can, in turn, develop department goals based upon the overall school goals. The success of any strategic plan can never be achieved without proper monitoring and assessing its progress, step 15. Therefore, it is critical that a process for evaluating the goals is established, which might consist of periodic review meetings and conducting districtwide update sessions with everyone.

Step 16 includes a review of the individuals' performance who are responsible for achieving the goals. This can be done through the performance appraisal process and periodic review meetings. Last, step 17 includes an evaluation of the strategic planning process through extensive follow-up sessions by the original strategic plan members. The evaluation might consist of what things went well, those things that did not go well, and ideas for improving the process in the strategic plan. Also in monitoring the goals of a strategic plan, it can be helpful to develop a spreadsheet listing each of the major goals, the key strategies for each goal, who is responsible, target completion date, metrics, and status. In this way the goals can easily be reviewed and comments can be written in the status section on the progress on each of the goals.

FORECASTING STUDENT ENROLLMENT

Human resources planning is an integral part of the strategic planning process and involves forecasting student enrollment for the school district, which helps administrators plan for future finances, facilities, and human resources. Forecasting student enrollment is like looking into a crystal ball but not having 100 percent accuracy. Administrators can use several methods to help predict student enrollment, such as quantitative statistical analysis and qualitative techniques. Quantitative statistics involve calculating the number of children in an elementary school district and determining the number likely to enroll in high school. Specific trends in elementary school enrollment over two- to four-year periods of time can be used to help predict enrollment trends. In addition, feedback from local realtors and statistics from the planning commissions of local municipalities can provide statistics on housing trends and residency.

Qualitative measures consists of administrators using inductive analysis to make conclusions based upon discussions with people through the local chamber of commerce and identifying potential new businesses coming or leaving the area, residential and commercial developments that are being planned, the general economy in the area, and geographical potential for expansion. For example, some school districts may be within a community that is landlocked or has older residents with decreasing numbers of children in school. Also, new emerging communities that have high growth and new residential and commercial developments can provide valuable clues as to the direction of enrollment trends. However all this information must be perceived with caution in that a community may be rapidly growing but suddenly, due to economic reasons, the development can come to a halt, leaving school buildings empty and future plans for school expansion dormant.

The human resources planning strategy essentially involves matching the school's human resources needs with the projected student enrollment. Administrators must make a good-faith effort in determining this match in order to avoid shortages, overstaffing issues, or employing teachers who have the wrong certifications needed for the students. For example, if a community is experiencing a high growth in foreign immigrants, the necessity for bilingual and ESL programs may be more critical than other areas. Likewise, nothing may be worse for an administrator than to overstaff a district and then experience a drastic decline in enrollment. This may necessitate a reduction in force (RIF). Recent legislation regarding desegregation and affirmative action has supported other means than using seniority as the basis whenever possible (Ray, Baker, & Plowman, 2011). LAWS

RIF ✓

SUCCESSION PLANNING

Succession planning is a common practice in identifying and securing internal and external people to fill key administrative leadership positions within the organization (Citrin & Ogden, 2010). This process can be one of the most valuable ways to ensure that human resource needs are met. Generally succession planning, or sometimes called replacement planning, is used for identifying successors for key administrative and staff positions. Oliver Wendall Holmes once stated, "The great thing in this world is not so much where we stand as in what direction we are going." The whole essence of succession planning is to be able to look into the future and ascertain which key positions need to be replaced. The succession planning process ensures that there is a successful transition of a candidate for a key position for the eventual retirement or unexpected separation of the incumbent from the position. More simply stated, having a viable succession plan in place in the event of an unfortunate or abrupt departure of a key person can help weather the transition period, maintain operational continuity, and ensure the successful selection of a replacement in a timely manner (Berlin, 2009).

Generally it is important that the superintendent of the school district establish a succession plan working with the school board. There needs to be a culture of honesty, trust, and mutual respect among members because inherent conflicts and misunderstanding are natural during this process. Therefore the necessity of self-examination, critical analysis of current performance, spirited discussions, and candidness are hallmarks in balancing the multiplicity of viewpoints that can commonly occur. The succession plan should be an ongoing and dynamic process that is regularly updated. It isn't something that should be viewed as a one-time exercise. The process can also serve as a useful process for self-examination, assessment of organizational current and future needs, and continuous improvement.

The succession planning process often begins by identifying possible candidates for selected positions to be filled. It is important to determine the future needs of the organization and having the end in sight versus focusing on past needs. Administrators who work collectively with an incumbent are more likely to establish a successful plan that is right for the future needs of the organization (Kleinsorge, 2010). In other words, if a key person is replaced, the dynamics of the administrative team may be impacted due to the varying skill sets that all the team members and the incumbent have. Some typical questions for thoughtful reflection include:

- Is there an up-to-date job description and set of core competencies for the position?
- What are mutual expectations of the school board and administrative leadership team?
- What are the major responsibilities for an ideal person in this position (versus the current job responsibilities of the position, which might have evolved based upon the skills and talents of the incumbent, existing administrative team members, political dynamics, and organizational needs)?

- Who could be an immediate interim leader, and has he or she been notified in the event of an incumbent's departure?
- Has a key administrator been identified who could manage the transition during the time before replacing the incumbent?
- Has a developmental plan been initiated to help prepare the interim leader for the position?
- Have all potential issues been identified that need to be stabilized during the transition period upon an incumbent's abrupt departure that will ensure operational continuity?

"Steps in Completing the Succession Planning Process" outlines the steps for the succession planning process. The first step involves ensuring that a current *job description* is in place. The job description should be updated to include the organizational role; essential duties and responsibilities; qualifications and requirements; and desired certificates, licenses, or registrations needed for the position. For example, a key position might be the business manager of a school district, principal, assistant superintendent for research and instructional development, or curriculum specialist.

The second step involves ensuring that the *core competencies*, which include performance skills, knowledge, and dispositions, have been developed for the key position. Generally these core competencies involve leadership and administrative skills as well as the actual functional/technical skills needed in the position. For example, if the core competencies for a position of an assistant superintendent for research and instructional development were completed, there would be specific leadership and management skills needed to work with people as well as the technical expertise of understanding research and statistical analysis.

Steps in Completing the Succession Planning Process
1. Develop a Current Job Description for the Incumbent Position.
   - Organizational role
   - Essential duties and responsibilities
   - Qualifications and requirements
   - Desired certificates, licenses, or registrations
2. Identify Core Competencies (Skills, Knowledge, and Dispositions).
   - Leadership and administrative skills
   - Functional/technical skills

CORE COMPETENCIES: PERF SKILLS, KNOWL, DISPOSITION

3. Determine School Board Expectations.
4. Identify and Assess Candidates for the Incumbent's Position.
5. Provide Development Plan for Internal Candidates.
6. Identify Promotability of Internal Candidates (Determine Anticipated Timeframe).

Step 3 involves working with the school board to ensure that there are agreed-upon *expectations* for the succession plan. Often a school board may work with an outside consultant to help facilitate the process and provide outside expertise and consultation.

Step 4 involves identifying and assessing *internal* and *external candidates* for the incumbent's position. Internal interim candidates should also be identified. This will help to ensure a smooth transition in the event of an abrupt departure of an incumbent.

Steps 5 includes identifying and providing a *developmental plan* for internal candidates for the position. The promotability of the candidate, step 6, should be determined along with an anticipated timeframe from which the candidate could be ready to assume the position.

Core Competencies of an Administrative Leadership Position
1. Strategic Focus. Is action-oriented, a visionary, proactive, anticipates the future, is innovative and energetic, and recognizes and seizes opportunities.
2. Financial Management. Has good business acumen, competent financial abilities, and budget management skills; experience with resource planning; and ability to review reports.
3. Leadership Skills. Holds people accountable, delegates, mentors, makes good decisions, has composure, motivates staff and students, has courage, and is approachable.
4. Teamwork. Is collaborative, a motivator, trustworthy, fosters open dialogue, builds spirit and commitment to staff and students, and manages conflict.
5. Communications. Is a good listener; has good verbal, nonverbal, and written communication skills; has good presentation skills; and meeting management experience.
6. Student Focus. Has respect, understanding, and good sensitivity to all students.

resources: people

7. Ethics and Integrity. Conducts self with high ethics and integrity; adheres to school's values, beliefs, and mission; and understands essential school law and policies.

8. Instruction and Curriculum. Understands critical aspects of instruction and curriculum.

9. Problem Solving. Solves difficult problems with effective solutions, has good analytical skills, and is a forward thinker and a good decision maker.

10. Time Management. Demonstrates effective planning and organizing skills and can martial resources (people, technology, materials) to get the job done.

11. Technology Expertise. Is proficient in information technology, has experience with school software, and uses technology at a high rate of proficiency.

12. Community Resourcefulness. Understands value and works with community and professional and business organizations in supporting the school.

There are several core competencies that can be identified for a key administrative leadership position. While these core competencies may vary, many of them can be common for any leadership position. The list "Core Competencies of an Administrative Leadership Position" shows an example of a set of core competencies for an administrative leadership position. Some of the essential competencies include having a strategic focus, business acumen, leadership and management skills, time management expertise, as well as problem-solving and communication skills. When the set of core competencies has been completed, it is then important to identify potential candidates to replace the incumbent and to complete a checklist that can be filed and used when necessary. The checklist might also include the following items:

- Promotability. Is the candidate ready to assume the position now or how many years into the future?
- Gap Analysis. The candidate should be evaluated based upon what specific gaps and core competencies are deficient and need to be developed.
- Career Development Plan. Once the gaps have been identified, then specific developmental actions should be completed for the candidate.

GAP ANALYSIS - deficiencies, dvpt

- Assigned Mentor. An assigned mentor within the organization should also be responsible for completing the succession planning process and working with the candidates.

The journey in establishing an effective succession plan can be rewarding in many ways: promoting a robust discussion, building honesty and trust, reexamining expectations, assessing performance, brainstorming alternatives for organizational structure and initiatives, and identifying suitable candidates who can lead the school organization in the future. Ultimately, the end result should be a structured and viable succession plan that ensures operational continuity and promoting a diverse workplace.

EMPLOYMENT LAWS

There are a myriad of federal and state laws and executive orders that impact human resource planning and employment (Hirsh & Kornrich, 2008). These laws cover a wide range of employment practices ranging from planning human resources, recruiting, interviewing and selection, writing job descriptions, compensation, placement and induction, career development, mentoring practices, professional development, employee evaluation, collective bargaining, managing conflict, handling grievances, and termination and RIF (see exhibit 1.1).

While there are many federal laws impacting education, there are also specific laws unique to individual states and school district policies. While federal laws tend to trump state and local laws, all of these laws must be understood and practiced by administrators. Also state laws and regulations generally specify certification and licensing regulations. Local school boards may establish higher standards than state regulations but generally cannot legally establish lower standards. An administrator must be well informed and seek local counsel in understanding the interrelationship of federal, state, and local school board laws and regulations.

For example, school boards may have the authority to set policy as long as the policy does not conflict with state laws. Also, there may be state laws that are not clearly defined by federal laws and statutes. For example, the State of Illinois added anti-sexual orientation discrimination to the Illinois Human Rights Act. Essentially this act states that it is unlawful to discriminate against sexual orientation as defined as "Actual or perceived heterosexuality, homo-

Law	Basic Description
Equal Pay Act of 1963	Prohibits pay discrimination against males and females who perform equal work that is substantially the same.
Title VII, Civil Rights Act of 1964 as amended	Prohibits discrimination on the basis of race; color; religion; national origin; gender, pregnancy, or childbirth; and retaliation.
Age Discrimination in Employment Act (ADEA) of 1967	Protects people who are forty or older from age discrimination or retaliation for filing a complaint.
Occupational Safety and Health (OSH) Act of 1970	Enforces standards for workplace safety and health to prevent work-related injuries, illnesses, and death. Provides regulatory safety guidelines to ensure safe work environment.
Title IV, Education Amendments of 1972	Prohibits discrimination against males and females in activities and programs receiving federal funding and grants.
Sections 501 and 505, Rehabilitation Act of 1973	Prohibits discrimination against qualified disabled people who can perform the major functions of a job and affirmative action to employ and promote qualified disabled people.
Vietnam-Era Veterans' Readjustment Act of 1974	Requires employers with federal contracts to provide affirmative action for Vietnam-era veterans to prevent discrimination for disabled Vietnam War veterans.
Pregnancy Discrimination Act of 1978	Provides equal employment opportunity protection for pregnant women and new mothers that they be treated like any other disability for employment matters.
Title VII, Section 1604, Sexual Harassment Act, 1980	Prohibits unwelcome sexual advances, requests for sexual favors, and other verbal or physical conduct of a sexual nature that creates a hostile or offensive work environment.
Title I, Americans with Disabilities Act (ADA) of 1990 Family and Medical Leave Act (FMLA) of 1993	Protects disabled people from employment discrimination or retaliation for filing a complaint. Requires employers to provide male and female employees up to twelve weeks a year in unpaid leave for qualified medical and family illness, military situations, pregnancy, foster care and adoption, or personal serious illness.

EXHIBIT 1.1

Major Federal and EEOC Laws and Executive Orders
Source: U.S. EEOC, www.eeoc.gov/laws, 2011

sexuality, bisexuality or general related identity, whether or not traditionally associated with the person's designated sex at birth" (Illinois Department of Human Rights, 2011). This addition to the Human Rights Act has created controversy within many public schools and local school board opinions regarding sexuality and employment practices within a school district. State laws may also provide different employment work and compensation safeguards for teachers and staff. For example, some states forbid school districts from waiving their rights granted by state law in matters concerning housing, compensation, cost of living adjustments, and contractual placement of teachers. Understanding the many federal and state laws is critical to reduce potential legal vulnerability for the school district, distress, and financial burden (Morgan & Vardy, 2009).

Many of the federal laws have originated based upon societal movements (Huffman, Cohen, & Pearlman, 2010). During the late 1800s, there were little federal laws that protected employees in the workplace. However, the Human Relations Era began in the 1930s, which strongly influenced the passage of several federal legislative acts. For example, in 1935 the National Labor Relations Act (NLRA) was established to prohibit discrimination against union members and employment and apprenticeship practices. There have been many additions to the Fair Labor Standards Act since 1938. Many of these provisions relate to child labor law, minimum wage requirements, overtime provisions, meals and breaks, travel, training, as well as additional guidelines for exempt employees.

The Labor Management Relations Act (LMRA) was established in 1947. This act, which is also known as the Taft-Hartley Act, is significant in outlining specific employment practices. This act is an offshoot to the original NLRA and contains additional provisions and guidelines regarding employees' right to free speech and collection of union dues. Also during this time, the Federal Mediation Conciliation Service (FMCS) was established to help resolve management and union disagreements.

EQUAL EMPLOYMENT OPPORTUNITY COMMISSION

As an outgrowth of the civil rights movement of the 1960s, the Equal Employment Opportunity Commission (EEOC) was established by Title VII of the 1964 Civil Rights Act. The original act prohibits discrimination on the basis of race, color, relation, national origin, and gender. This law covers all aspects of employment, including planning, hiring, supervising, compensation, job classification, promotions, training, and retirement and termination. While the Civil Rights Act primarily covers all employers and public and private institutions with fifteen or more employees, the act provides the basis for bringing litigation against institutions that practiced discriminatory acts. This federal law creates protected classes of employees, which mainly consist of women, African Americans, Asians, Hispanics, Indians, and Eskimos.

Subsequently, amendments have been made to the act that include protecting individuals above forty, disabled people, and pregnant women. Also, in 1978, the EEOC adopted other guidelines to protect claims of reverse discrimination practices as an outgrowth of affirmative action. Essentially, the act stated that organizations should avoid selection policies that have an adverse impact on hiring or employment opportunities because of race, gender, or ethnicity unless there is an organizational necessity for the practice.

The penalties associated with Civil Rights Act violations can be severe. The law allows individuals who have been discriminated against to seek compensatory and punitive damages for both willful and intentional discrimination acts. Compensatory damages generally involve harm to an employee for pain and emotional suffering. Punitive damages can be assessed against an employer, which serves as punishment and a deterrent for others. There are some limitations for judgment awards depending upon the size of an organization. In addition to the EEOC, violations of discrimination are also enforced and judgments can be awarded by state human rights commissions. For example, the State of Illinois has a Department of Human Rights Commission, which is responsible for protecting individuals from discriminatory practices.

Both the EEOC and state human rights commissions have the authority to assess monetary penalties, and both of these agencies have established time frames in which a claim can be filed. For example, the State of Illinois typically allows for 180 days from the occurrence, and the EEOC allows 300 days. Not only can an organization incur financial costs for acts of discrimination, but they can also incur significant emotional pain, legal costs, work disruption, and wasted time and resources defending claims. Therefore, organizations are wise to follow legal practices and avoid claims of discrimination.

The Equal Pay Act of 1963 is an outgrowth to the Fair Labor Standards Act. This law prohibits compensation discrimination for people who have the same skills and experiences and are performing the same job. However, there

can be several exceptions to pay differences, such as bonuses for higher per-
formances, seniority, merit, working conditions, geographic differences, and
quality and quantity of work. The law primarily serves to protect differences
in pay between men and women who are substantially doing the same work
and have the same qualifications, performance, and seniority.

The Occupational Safety and Health Act (OSHA) was established in 1970.
This act includes mandatory safety and health standards for all employers.
The objective of the act is to prevent occupational injuries and illnesses by
enforcing standards of workplace safe practices. The law is enforced by the
Occupational Safety and Health Administration (OSHA), a division of the
U.S. Department of Labor (DOL). This agency, in addition to implementing
investigations for work-related injuries, also initiates proactive inspections of
organizations when there is a possible hazard or danger to people. This law
has had a major impact on school district facilities and requires administrators to ensure that the facilities are safe and do not impose health risks and
illnesses to staff and students. The agency has the power to impose monetary
fines and require facility improvements. The agency also provides significant
safety regulations involving permissible exposure limits, personal protec-
tive equipment, hazard communications, safety management, blood-borne
pathogens, evacuations, exposure to asbestos, and in some cases mandatory
training for safety and health practices.

Title IV of the Education Amendments Act of 1972 prohibits discrimination on the basis of gender for educational programs by recipients of federal
financial assistance. The act states that "no persons in the United States shall,
on the basis of sex, be excluded from participating in, be denied the benefits
of, or be subjected to discrimination under any program or activity receiving
Federal financial assistance" (U.S. Equal Employment Opportunity Commission, 2011). This law requires school districts to maintain internal procedures
for federal grants and to resolve complaints of discrimination. In addition,
Title IV also applies to programs of a school district regardless of whether the
program is federally funded.

The Rehabilitation Act of 1973 serves to promote equality for employees
with disabilities. This law requires that employers take affirmative action
to recruit, hire, and promote qualified disabled people. The law serves to
protect disabled persons who can perform the main functions of the job
with reasonable accommodations. While the law has good intentions, some
administrators may have difficulty interpreting exactly what "reasonable ac-

commodations" means. The law does not mandate that accommodations be made if it imposes a significant hardship or monetary expense that is unreasonable for a school district. However, in most cases administrators can accommodate disabled employees through actions, such as modifying work schedules and providing ergonomic devices and other special equipment or modifications to support a disabled person in performing the primary functions of a job. Examples of accommodations might include installing entrance ramps for people in wheelchairs, special seat cushions for back pathologies, wrist splints for accumulative trauma disorders, and special lighting for people with eye-related diseases. It should be noted that a school district is not required to hire a disabled person who is less qualified than nondisabled people. The intention of the law it to prevent discrimination against disabled people who can perform the major functions of the job.

The Vietnam-Era Veterans' Readjustment Act of 1974 followed the Vietnam War. This act mandates that employers take affirmative action to recruit, hire, and promote Vietnam War veterans and disabled veterans. Definitions of veterans of the Vietnam War include U.S. ground, naval, or air service military people who served during the period of 1964 through 1975. The regulations of the law are intended to prevent employers from discriminating against protected Vietnam War veterans. This law mainly impacts contractors or subcontractors receiving federal funds. In addition, employers are required to keep records for at least two years. However employers who have less than 150 employees are only required to maintain records for one year. Examples of records include job descriptions, job advertisements, interview notes, applications, resumes, employment policies, human resource files, and any related employment forms and records.

The Pregnancy Discrimination Act of 1978 provides protection for pregnant women and new mothers to ensure that they be treated like disabled persons for employment matters. This act is an amendment to the Title VII Civil Right Act and impacts organizations with at least fifteen employees. This law would provide protection for pregnant women in hiring, promotion, and terminating practices.

The Family and Medical Leave Act (FMLA) of 1993 prohibits discrimination to male and female employees who desire to take twelve weeks of unpaid leave because of the birth of a child, adoption or foster care of a child, or caring for a family member who has a serious health condition. This law is administered by the Wage and Hour Division of the U.S. DOL. The law supports people who have qualified medical and family situations, leaving decisions to the discretion of the employer. Interpretation of the law is not always clear cut, and while guidelines have been provided by the federal agency, questions regarding what medical situations qualify remain. For example, the federal FMLA does not recognize many part-time workers who desire unpaid leave or certain employers with less than fifty employees. Also, employees who desire to take unpaid time off for illnesses of relatives, pets, personal short-term illness, or other routine medical care are generally excluded. Other related FMLA state statutes may apply as well. For example, the State of California recognizes domestic partners and children of domestic partners. Connecticut, on the other hand, recognizes parents-in-law of civil union partners, and the State of Hawaii recognizes grandparents of employees.

The EEOC included a sexual harassment amendment in 1980 to the Title VII Civil Rights Act. This law prohibits sexual harassment in the workplace. The law states that *sexual harassment* involves "unwelcome sexual advances, requests for sexual favors, and other verbal or physical conduct of a sexual nature—when such conduct has the purpose or effect of unreasonably interfering with an individual's work performance or creating an intimidating, hostile or offensive working environment" (U.S. Equal Employment Opportunity Commission, 2011).

There are several types of sexual harassment discrimination in this amendment (Perry, 2008). *Adverse impact discrimination* involves the unintentional actions that have negative or detrimental effects against a person or group of people. This discrimination might involve requiring certain height requirements that could unintentionally discriminate against people of a certain ethnicity. *Adverse treatment discrimination* involves the intentional act of treating people differently. An example of this discrimination could be asking different interview questions for men versus women during an employment interview. *Retaliation* is an intentional discrimination that occurs when an employer commits an adverse action against the employee because he or she has complained about discrimination or filed a discrimination claim. Another type of sexual discrimination is called *quid pro quo*. This harassment (or called "this for that" or "in exchange for") entails requesting sexual favors in exchange for some type of employment benefit. An example of quid pro quo might be a school administrator requesting sexual favors from a teacher in exchange for a good performance rating or promotion. A type of sexual harassment discrimination that addresses *environmental sexual harassment* is called *hostile working environment*. This type of harassment involves any unreasonable actions that interfere with an employee's work performance and that have a sexual basis. Examples might include verbal, physical, and visual sexual actions; patently offensive conduct; harassment of individuals because of their gender; displaying inappropriate sexual pictures; physically touching people; or sending sexually based content e-mails. Sexual harassment complaints have significantly increased over the past years. School administrators are required to post sexual harassment policies, conduct investigations when complaints have been received, take action against offenders, provide training for employees, and provide an employee complaint mechanism or grievance system. Many state laws have similar provisions to the federal Title VII amendment. Sexual harassment discrimination has become a complex law and requires school administrators to consult legal counsel.

The Age Discrimination in Employment Act (ADEA) of 1967 was designed to prohibit age discrimination for employees over forty years of age in planning, recruiting, selection, training, promoting, transferring, compensating, and other practices of employment. The intention of the law is to prevent companies from discharging or refusing to hire older workers based upon their age (Jusko, 2011). In 1986 this act was amended to prohibit discrimination in retirement for people above forty years of age. An example of this law would include a school district that forced a competent sixty-year-old teacher to retire against his or her will in order to hire a twenty-two-year-old teacher in order to save money for the school district. It should be noted that this law protects people who are forty years of age or older but does not protect people who are under the age of forty. It is never a good practice to hire or fire people based upon age rather than performance factors and needs of the school. Also because of this law, many school districts have offered early retirement programs in an effort to encourage retirement and reduce costs.

The Americans with Disabilities Act (ADA) of 1990 Title I was established to prevent discrimination against disabled individuals who can perform the essential functions of a job with reasonable accommodations. This law generally applies to employers who have fifty or more employees. This law has had significant impact on school districts given that it covers such a wide range of medical conditions, such as HIV, mental illnesses, learning disabilities, alcohol and drug addiction, and other physical ailments. This law is executed under the EEOC and was subsequently amended to prohibit school districts from discrimination regardless of the number of employees.

SUMMARY

The primary goal of human resources planning is to forecast the future needs of an organization and to ensure that all resources are obtained. Proper planning entails understanding the goals of the organization, anticipating changes in staffing, understanding and staying current with federal and state laws and local district policies, and working with school administrators to match future needs and current organizational resources with future resources.

There are many strategies used to help plan and predict resources, such as strategic planning, succession planning, and human resource forecasting, to satisfy future organizational, financial, facilities, and human resource needs. Proper planning allows for all administrators to develop a framework to recruit, select, hire, mentor, and develop future people to meet staffing needs. There is no one strategy that can guarantee a perfect prediction of all human resource needs since the planning process is a dynamic one and must adapt to the changing needs of the organization. Therefore, the human resource planning process is matching the needs of a school with available people. The bottom line is that the "trains must leave on time," and all operations and staffing need to be in place to best service the educational needs of the students.

CASE STUDY

Washington Magnet School—Creating a Ninety-Day Entry Plan

Washington School is a magnet school in an urban environment serving about 1,600 students from early childhood to eighth grade. The school specializes in the language arts and is recognized throughout the city as being a good academic institution. The school is searching for a new principal since the recent termination of the last principal for poor performance.

There is a myriad of problems at the school, which include:

1. Low test scores;
2. Low staff morale;
3. High attrition rate of teachers;
4. Frequent complaints from parents regarding curriculum, instruction, and school policies;
5. Several recent filings of sexual harassment complaints against female teachers by male teachers; and
6. A lack of financial accountability and controls.

COMMUNICATION

In addition to these issues, the district has made several recent policy changes that have impacted the school. These policies will increase the student enrollment at the school over the next two years. This increase in students will put a strain on the school's capacity, and there will be a need to expand the facilities of the school in order to accommodate this increased enrollment. Also, additional staff must be hired to accommodate these new students.

The school board is in the process of hiring a new principal who could start immediately to address these issues and plan for the future. You are a candidate for the principal position, and the school board has asked you to prepare a "ninety-day entry plan" outlining what you would do as a new principal during your first ninety days on the job. The school board would like for you to prepare this written, comprehensive ninety-day entry plan and present it at the next board meeting. This should include detailed human resource planning, communication, facilities, legal concerns, staff morale, budget and finance, instruction and curriculum, enrollment projection, and any other factors deemed important.

EXERCISES AND DISCUSSION QUESTIONS

1. Develop a comprehensive strategic plan for your school following the steps outlined in this chapter.
2. Using your school as an example, prepare a succession plan for the assistant principal position.
3. Interview a school administrator, and outline the process for human resources planning that is being used.
4. Interview a school administrator, and identify some of the major legal issues confronting the school, including recent complaints and lawsuits.
5. List and describe at least six different EEOC laws or executive orders.
6. Outline the grievance or complaint procedure for a staff member to follow in filing a sexual harassment claim at the school.
7. Explain the history and process of the EEOC.
8. List and explain the laws that protect people on the basis of race, sex, religion, national origin, age, and disability.
9. Research and list some laws unique to your state and how they support federal laws.

REFERENCES

Berlin, L. (2009). Public school law: What does it mean in the trenches? *Phi Delta Kappan*, 90 (10), 733–36.

Citrin, J., & Ogden, D. (2010). Succeeding at succession. *Harvard Business Review*, 88 (11), 29–31.

Earley, P., Weindling, D., Bubb, S., & Glenn, M. (2009). Future leaders: The way forward? *School Leadership & Management*, 29 (3), 295–306.

Hirsh, C., & Kornrich, S. (2008). The context of discrimination: Workplace conditions, institutional environments, and sex and race discrimination charges. *American Journal of Sociology*, 113 (5), 1394–432.

Huffman, M., Cohen, P. N., & Pearlman, J. (2010). Engendering change: Organizational dynamics and workplace gender desegregation, 1975–2005. *Administrative Science Quarterly*, 55 (2), 255–77.

Illinois Department of Human Rights. (2011). 775 ILCS 5 Human Rights Act. http://www.ilga.gov/legislation/ilcs/ilcs3.asp?ActID=2266&ChapterID=64

Jusko, J. (2011). EEOC underestimates impact of ADA Amendments Act. *Industry Week*, 260 (5), 18.

Kleinsorge, R. (2010). Expanding the role of succession planning. T+D, 64 (4), 66–69.

Marler, J. H. (2009). Making human resources strategic by going to the net: Reality or myth? *International Journal of Human Resource Management*, 20 (3), 515–27.

Morgan, J., & Vardy, F. (2009). Diversity in the workplace. *American Economic Review*, 99 (1), 472–85.

Perry, P. (2008). Just say no to harassment. *Restaurant Hospitality*, 92 (11), 44–48.

Ray, J., Baker, L., & Plowman, D. (2011). Organizational mindfulness in business schools. *Academy of Management Learning & Education*, 10 (2), 188–203.

Thompson, K. (2010). How strategic is the school-based planning for leadership succession? *International Studies in Educational Administration (Commonwealth Council for Educational Administration & Management [CCEAM])*, 38 (1), 98–113.

U.S. Equal Employment Opportunity Commission. (2011). Laws and guidance. www.eeoc.gov/laws.

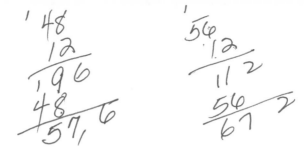

2

Recruitment and Selection

OBJECTIVES

At the conclusion of this chapter, you will be able to:

1. Understand recruitment strategies and procedures used by school administrators (ELCC 3.1; ISLLC 3).
2. Differentiate between federal and state laws that impact recruitment and employment practices (ELCC 6.1, 6.2, 6.3; ISLLC 6).
3. Understand reasons why candidates select a school for employment (ELCC 3.1; ISLLC 3).
4. Describe the typical selection process used by school districts (ELCC 3.1, 3.3; ISLLC 3).
5. Understand different interviewing techniques used for selecting the best candidates for positions (ELCC 2.1, 3.3; ISLLC 3).

RECRUITING APPLICANTS

Human resources recruiting is a critical part of the job of the school administrator. Recruiting the best candidates to fill job positions is a dynamic process and a never-ending one. Throughout the decades in the United States, school districts have experienced dramatic shifts in student enrollment (Balter & Duncombe, 2008). For example, in the 1960s the student population significantly increased and then began a gradual decline during the 1970s, reflecting the changing population age in the United States (Kollie, 2008).

Although the United States experienced a recession in 2008, most public school districts continued to employ large numbers of teachers largely because of increased federal stimulus funding. In the 2012 school year, nearly 50 million students were attending public elementary and secondary schools. Nearly 35 million of these students were enrolled in pre-kindergarten through eighth grade, and nearly 15 million were enrolled in high school. Another 6 million students were enrolled in private schools (National Center for Education Statistics, 2012).

Without a doubt education is a big business. It is estimated that public school districts hired over 3 million teachers in 2012. This represents a student–teacher ratio of 15.5:1. This ratio compares to a student–teacher ratio of 16.0:1 in the year 2000. Private schools are experiencing significantly lower teacher-to-student ratios. For example, in the fall of 2011, the National Center for Education Statistics estimated that the private school student–teacher ratio was 12.9:1, which represents a significantly lower ratio than in public education (National Center for Education Statistics, 2012).

Although there have been increases in the teacher employment, school districts vary from one another in the number of teachers being hired. Many school districts are experiencing financial difficulties and are not recruiting or hiring many, if any, teachers. Much of the fiscal condition of a school district and subsequent hiring practices are impacted by the amount of local community tax and state funding. Also, some teachers who planned for early retirement have prolonged their retirement given the economic downturn and need to support family or maintain a desired standard of living. For example, during the 1980s large numbers of teachers retired and created many vacancies for new recruits.

During the recession of 2008 and subsequent years, there have been fewer retirements, which has caused a decrease in hiring of new teachers. The recruitment process is a proactive one. Administrators need to predict job vacancies and fill them with the intention of securing long-term employees. The recruitment process is also expensive for a school district, and hiring the wrong teachers only serves to increase these costs as well as contribute to lower morale and operating inefficiencies. Therefore, school administrators need to take the recruitment process very seriously and strive to select the best candidates for their school district. Likewise, applying for job vacancies can be a very competitive and time-consuming process for applicants.

If an applicant is not selected for an interview or for employment, he or she may feel that there was discrimination involved and can react by filing a complaint or lawsuit against the school district. Therefore, administrators need to practice all safeguards to ensure that the recruiting process is professional and compliant with all federal, state, and district laws and policies (Mason, 2010).

KEY

Compliance

Reasons Why Applicants Select a School for Employment

1. School is close to home.
2. Geographic location.
3. Working environment.
4. Academic reputation of school.
5. Supportive administrators.
6. Compensation and benefits.
7. Promotion and growth opportunities.
8. Personal identity with school.
9. Specialization of the school.
10. Religious affiliation of a private school.
11. Culture at the school.
12. Desirable working hours.

TYPES OF EDUCATIONAL PROGRAMS

There are many reasons why applicants apply to a school other than compensation. "Reasons Why Applicants Select a School for Employment" lists several of the reasons why applicants are motivated to work at a selected school. Sometimes people may assume that the main purpose for a teacher applying to a school is pay and benefits. However, this is not always the case. People are motivated to work for both extrinsic and intrinsic reasons (Odden, 2011).

Extrinsic factors are tangible items, such as pay, benefits, work conditions, and supervisions practices. Intrinsic factors are intangible things, such as appreciating the academic mission of the school, feeling connected with the school, interesting work, receiving full appreciation for work, and the love for the actual work itself. These factors can vary from one school to another. A private school with a strong religious culture can attract applicants for employment if they value this environment. However, an applicant might be motivated to work at an urban school with poor working conditions and high disciplinary problems if there is good compensation and they value money as a major priority. Some people are more motivated by money rather than other factors. Some applicants may be partial toward the diversity and ethnicity of the school student population. Also, a school that has a largely Hispanic student population may attract applicants who are Hispanic.

Administrators need to be sensitive to the type of student population, ethnicity, and religious affiliation when recruiting the best qualified teachers for the school (Anyaso, 2008). Administrators need to understand the motivation of applicants and to have a realistic discussion with applicants to ensure that there is a good fit between the applicants and the school. From a finance standpoint, administrators need to recognize these intrinsic and extrinsic motivators when planning school budgets and negotiating compensation contracts.

The recruitment planning process consists of several steps (see "Steps in Recruitment Planning"). The recruiting process begins with developing a comprehensive *strategic plan*, which includes the goals of the school. These goals should determine the staffing needs for school. For example, if the goals are to promote English as a second language (ESL) and bilingual programs, then qualified applicants will need to be secured. Also, if the school is experiencing excessive student disciplinary problems, then a disciplinary dean position may need to be created.

Steps in Recruitment Planning
1. Develop strategic plan and organizational goals.
2. Forecast potential vacancies and budget.
3. Establish job analysis and certification requirements.
4. Develop job descriptions.
5. Obtain school board approval.
6. Post internal and external job openings.
7. Begin recruiting applicants.
8. Establish a pool of candidates.

The job positions of a school should be based upon the anticipated educational and organizational needs of the school as determined by the school board. Once a position has been forecasted, a complete *job analysis* needs to be done. A job analysis outlines the knowledge, skills, dispositions, and tasks needed in the position. The job analysis is used as a foundation to create a job description. A job description should clearly outline the duties and responsibilities of a position and should conform to the Americans with Disabilities Act (ADA) guidelines. The ADA requires that all job descriptions provide the necessary requirements for a position in order to understand the functions of the job for disabled applicants. A typical job description would contain topics such as:

1. Title of the position and whether exempt or nonexempt status;
2. Summary job description;
3. Essential duties and responsibilities;
4. Special qualification requirements;
5. Education and certification requirements;
6. Special skills required (language, mathematical reasoning ability, etc.);
7. Certificates, licenses, and registrations;
8. Physical demands; and
9. Work environment conditions.

A *job description* needs to be thorough and complete. Applicants need to know the essential duties and responsibilities, including the physical demands and conditions of the work environment. For example, an applicant should know how many pounds of weight he or she may be required to lift; amount of standing, sitting, or stooping; and hearing and visual qualities required for a job. All of this information is needed to meet ADA requirements. These requirements also serve as a basis for determining *reasonable accommodations* that are necessary to enable individuals with disabilities to perform the essential functions of the job.

For example, if an employee needs to work in outside weather conditions for extended periods of time or in dirty or noisy work environments, these requirements should be specific and clearly outlined. Every job is different. The job of a teacher in a classroom is going to be different than a building engineer or a groundskeeper. For example, if a bus driver is being hired, he or she may need to have a valid commercial driver's license and acceptable peripheral and distance vision, which may be different for a teacher. If a building engineer needs to be able to occasionally lift twenty-five pounds, this essential job function needs to be clearly outlined in the physical demands section. If an applicant is unable, due to physical disability, to lift these amounts, then he or she may be rejected as an applicant.

Therefore it is critical that administrators follow appropriate legal guidelines and seek legal counsel in administering the recruiting and selection process. Once the job descriptions have been completed and approved by the school board, the job openings can be posted. Some job openings might be first posted internally and then opened to the public. After posting the job openings, the recruiting process begins by creating a pool of candidates to interview.

Examples of Employment Recruitment Sources
1. Employee referrals
2. Electronic databases
3. Internet websites
4. District website
5. Job fairs
6. Employment agencies
7. Professional associations
8. Print media
9. Broadcast media
10. Educational institutions
11. Recruiting brochures
12. Unsolicited applicants and walk-ins

There are many sources for recruiting teachers and staff. "Examples of Employment Recruitment Sources" lists typical employment recruiting sources. One of the best sources of potential applicants is _personal referrals_ from employees. While some people may think that employees may be eager to recommend a friend or relative for a job, they may have second thoughts if the person is poorly qualified and they have to work with this person. Many people will not compromise their values and recommend a person unless they feel the applicant is highly qualified and is a good fit for the position and organization. Referrals by employees are often desirable since it is one of the least costly sources of recruiting. One of the best ways for applicants to be referred to a school for employment is to get to know the teachers and administrators at the school. This often can be done through participation in professional associations, student teaching assignments, and substitute teaching where they have an opportunity to get to work with these people.

In the corporate world, sometimes employers are given a referral bonus for recommending people who are hired. This practice is not common in school institutions, but the referring employee may receive intangible rewards through recognition and satisfaction of recommending qualified applicants. Many school districts also have established policies and procedures regarding nepotism and referring applicants as potential candidates.

The advent of technology has dramatically changed the recruiting process. The use of electronic databases, Internet, and the school district websites are all very quick, convenient, and efficient sources for recruiting applicants. There are numerous job websites that can be utilized, such as educational associations, universities, employment search firms, and state department of education websites.

Other recruiting sources can range from attending job fairs to using employment agencies. The use of *employment agencies,* often called headhunters, is largely reserved for securing upper-level administrators. Use of employment agencies can be costly to the school district and can range from 10 to 30 percent of the employee's first-year salary. Some advantages to using employment agencies include a comprehensive screening of all applicants, extensive completion of background checks, and professional consultation. Search firms can also be beneficial when trying to obtain hard-to-find candidates for a position.

Print and *broadcast media* continue to be used today, although to a lesser degree than the Internet. Advertisements can be placed in professional educational association print materials, such as newsletters, magazines, and journals. Some educational organizations include the Association for Supervision and Curriculum Development (ASCD), National Association of Elementary School Principals (NAESP), National Association of Secondary School Principals (NASSP), National School Boards Association (NSBA), and the American Association of School Personnel Administrators (AASPA). Some of these associations, such as American Association of School Administrators (AASA), actually produce a job bulletin. This bulletin offers free job searching and resume posting. It offers a section exclusively for job seekers and allows them to view all jobs in the bulletin, and new jobs are posted every week. There is also a special section for employers and recruiters that can be utilized to post positions, although there is a fee for the use of this service.

Another inexpensive source is the *unsolicited application*. Virtually every school district receives unsolicited job inquiries. This source can be much cheaper than the expense of advertising and attending job fairs and conferences. However, depending upon the district, the number of inquiries and applications can be voluminous. If a popular school district only has a few openings, it is not unusual to receive literally thousands of applications. This can be overwhelming for the human resources administrator in tracking and responding to all of these inquiries. Nevertheless, this can be a very valuable source of identifying good applicants for a vacancy.

Human resource administrators need to become proficient in developing a system for screening these applications. Search committees are often formed to help screen the qualified applicants. Also, administrative assistants are used to sort through applications, screen the applications, and select the ones that meet the qualifications of a job. For example, recruitment expenses can range from advertisement costs, travel, meals and lodging, convention registration fees, and time for participating in these events.

The recruitment process is one that is a necessity for all school districts in securing the best-qualified people to fulfill the needs of the organization. Following federal, state, and local district laws and policies is critical in ensuring that the recruiting process is compliant and nondiscriminatory. All administrators involved in the recruiting process should periodically evaluate the recruitment program. This evaluation may include the use of efficient resources, time and effort, cost per employee hired, and quality of the database system. The goal is to incorporate a continuous improvement process that is efficient and cost effective for recruiting best-qualified applicants for the school.

The entire planning and management of human resources can be integrated into one computer system called *Enterprise Resource Planning* (ERP). The ERP is a computer system that integrates internal and external administrative functions of human resources, finance, accounting, and operations into one database. ERPs are excellent systems for employees to calculate human resource costs, provide real-time data access, file and track employee information, administrative recordkeeping, contractual agreements with unions, and business functions of the organization.

Steps in the Interviewing Process
1. Gain approval for job position and establish budget. ✓
2. Establish a search committee.

3. Review federal and state interviewing laws.
4. Advertise job position.
5. Screen applicants.
6. Interview applicants.
7. Select the best candidate for job position.
8. Extend offer for employment.
9. Conduct background and reference checks.
10. Finalize mutual acceptance and documentation.

school dist have depts (handwritten annotation)

SELECTING APPLICANTS

The goal of the selection process is to interview and select the best-qualified applicant for a job position. Selecting a candidate can be a costly endeavor. The process requires a number of activities, such as planning, interviewing, screening, selecting, completing reference checks, and obtaining legal counsel (Actkinson, 2011). Therefore, school districts need to develop the most efficient selection process that is cost effective and maximizes the use of internal resources.

The interviewing process, if done right, is a comprehensive one. Much of the work for the interview takes place before and after the interview session. There can be an enormous amount of time and effort in the planning process alone. The process begins with the formation of a selection committee. This group may consist of the human resources administrator, school principal, and selected teachers or staff. Some administrators may feel that more participation adds to a higher quality selection process and the more likely all the employees will be inclined to accept the new employees.

Besides the search committee, sometimes stakeholders are involved in the selection process. The school board often approves vacancies and positions, and the central office administrators are generally responsible for the overall process. Also, teacher unions may have contractual agreements that impact the selection process.

The overall objective is to hire the best candidate for a position and to obtain employment longevity. The process fails when the wrong applicant is hired for a position or separates from the organization within a short amount of time. Once the selection committee has been formed, the members need to understand all pre-employment legal guidelines and review the application form, electronic databases, resumes, job requirements, and other materials for undertaking the screening and interview process (Bilimoria, 2010). Once the job description has been advertised, then applicants are generally required to complete the job application. Exhibit 2.1 shows a typical job application.

Prior to scheduling the interview sessions, the members of the screening committee need to thoroughly understand all the pre-employment laws that impact interviewing a candidate (Herreid, 2010). The members need to understand permissible and nonpermissible questions for the interviewing process (see exhibit 2.2). For example, many unacceptable applications list questions that are contrary to federal and state laws. It is generally unacceptable to ask a person's age or date of graduation from a school on the application form. These types of questions may violate federal, state, and EEOC laws since they may reveal a person's age and constitute age discrimination. Questions regarding if an applicant has been arrested are generally unacceptable. Some legal experts feel that there have been a disproportionate number of arrests of minorities in the United States. Therefore, if a school district were to use the number of arrests versus the number of convictions, they could be inadvertently discriminating against minority applicants, which may violate the Civil Rights Act. However, questions regarding if an applicant has been convicted of a crime are generally appropriate, especially when the nature of the business involves students. School administrators have a responsibility to keep the students safe and free from potential criminal acts. Generally speaking, felony convictions involving sex, drugs, and physical violence would disqualify an applicant from employment. A teacher would also not be able to obtain a state teaching license if convicted of these types of crimes. The nature of the crime conviction needs to be relevant to the job of the applicant. For example, if an applicant is applying for a job as a groundskeeper and has been convicted of the felony of tax evasion, rejecting the applicant on this basis may be illegal. However, if an applicant is applying for a business director position at a school district and has had a prior felony conviction for tax evasion or has filed for bankruptcy, he or she would undoubtedly be rejected.

The application for employment should always be reviewed and updated, if necessary, prior to beginning the search process to ensure current legal compliance. For example, statements that reveal an applicant's age, gender, ethnicity, religious creed, color, national origin, ancestry, or disability are generally unacceptable on the application.

In preparing for the interview it is generally advisable to write out the questions in advance and ask each applicant the same questions. This infor-

SAMPLE APPLICATION FOR EMPLOYMENT
APPLICANTS MAY BE TESTED FOR ILLEGAL DRUGS

DATE: _____

Name _____
       Last   First   Middle   Maiden

Present Address _____
       Number   Street   City   State   Zip

How Long? _____ Social Security No. _____

Telephone (   )_____ Are you 18 years or older?   Yes _____   No _____

Type of School	Name of School	Location (complete mailing address)	Number of Years Completed	Major/Degree & Certification
High School				
College				

Have you ever been convicted of a crime?   Yes _____   No _____   (please check yes or no)
If yes, explain number of conviction(s), nature of offense(s) leading to conviction(s), how recently such offence(s) was/were committed, sentence(s) imposed, and type(s) of rehabilitation. _____

CURRENT EMPLOYER				
Date Month and Year	Name and Address of Employer	Salary	Position	Reason for Leaving
From				
To				

FORMER EMPLOYERS (List Below Last Two Employers, Starting With Last One First)				
Date Month and Year	Name and Address of Employer	Salary	Position	Reason for Leaving
From				
To				
From				
To				

REFERENCES			
Name	Address	Phone	Years Acquainted

I certify the application information is true, and if I am employed I may be terminated if the information is found not true. I authorize the school district to investigate this information and check references, and I release the school district from all claims for obtaining such information. If hired, I will be an employee at will and can be terminated at any time.

_____   _____
            Signature   Date

EXHIBIT 2.1
Sample Application for Employment

Subject	Acceptable	Unacceptable
Name	Have you used any other names?	Has your name been changed by a court order?
Residence	What is your address?	Do you own or rent your home? How long have you lived at your residence?
Age	If hired, can you show proof of age? Are you over eighteen years of age?	Birthdate, age, dates of attendance or completion of elementary or high school? Questions that tend to identify applicants over age forty
Birthplace, Citizenship	Can you, after employment, submit verifications of your legal right to work in the United States? Are you legally authorized to work in the United States?	What is the birthplace of your parents and spouse? Are you a U.S. citizen? Can you produce naturalization papers prior to employment?
National Origin	What languages do you read, speak, or write? Can you speak, read, or write Spanish?	What is your mother's native language? Where did you learn to read, write, or speak a foreign language and English?
Sex, Marital Status, Family	What is the name and address of your parent or guardian if you are a minor? What is your gender (if it is a bona fide occupational qualification for the job)?	Questions about applicant's sex Questions that indicate applicant's marital status Number and/or ages of children or dependents and childcare Questions regarding pregnancy, child bearing, or birth control
Race, Color	Can you provide a photograph after you are hired? (Personal data required for federal governmental affirmative action after hired)	Questions as to applicant's race or color Questions regarding applicant's complexion or color of skin, eyes, or hair
Physical Condition, Handicap	Questions contingent on applicant passing a job-related physical examination Can you perform the functions of the job with or without reasonable accommodation?	Questions regarding applicant's general medical condition, state of health Questions regarding receipt of workers' compensation Do you have any physical disabilities or handicaps?

	Acceptable	Unacceptable
Religion	Statement by employer of regular days, hours, or shifts to be worked	Questions regarding applicant's religion Religious days observed Does your religion prevent you from working weekends or holidays?
Arrest, Criminal Record	Have you ever been convicted of a felony or a misdemeanor that resulted in imprisonment?	Have you ever been stopped by a police officer while driving? Have you ever been arrested?
Military Service	Questions regarding relevant skills acquired during applicant's U.S. military service	General questions regarding military service, such as dates and type of discharge Questions about reserve duty Questions regarding service in a foreign military
Organizations, Activities	Please list job-related organizations, clubs, professional societies, or other associations to which you belong (omitting race, religious creed, color, national origin, ancestry, sex, or age disclosure).	List all organizations, clubs, societies, and lodges to which you belong.
References	→ By whom were you referred for a position here? → Names of persons willing to provide professional and/or character references for applicant	Questions that disclose the applicant's race, color, names, creed, national origin, ancestry, physical handicap, medical condition, marital status, age, or sex
Emergency Notification	A request for the name and address of a person to be notified in an emergency is proper after you have been hired.	Relationship or ethnicity of person to contact in an emergency

EXHIBIT 2.2
Acceptable and Unacceptable Pre-Employment Questions

Adopted from Department of Fair Employment Housing. 01/86.2000. Guidelines for pre-emploment interview questions. www.msubillings.edu/careers/PDF/pre-empguidelines03.pdf

mation should also be documented and filed should there be an audit by a human rights agency or to defend against a claim of discrimination. There are different state and federal guidelines regarding how long the records should be kept, which is generally two to three years.

If information is needed in order to complete a background check, questions about an applicant's assumed name may be necessary and permissible. However, asking a person's maiden name may reveal a person's ethnicity or race and is generally not acceptable, nor is it needed for making a decision whether or not an applicant can perform the essential functions of the job. Also, asking questions about whether a name has been changed by a court order is generally unacceptable. For example, a parent may change the name of a child later in life or a person may change his or her name due to a divorce or to have a more common name.

During the interview session, asking questions of an applicant about their birthplace, parents, spouse, and other relatives is generally unacceptable since it may reveal a person's national origin. Generally in the United States, an applicant does not need to be a U.S. citizen to be employed. Rather, this person simply needs to be legally authorized to work in the country. It is necessary to obtain verification documents that a person is eligible to work in the country but only after an offer of employment has been extended. Questions such as "Can you produce naturalization papers prior to employment?" or "Were you born in the United States?" are generally unacceptable.

An area that is less clear cut involves hiring a bilingual or ESL teacher. The school board may desire to hire a teacher who has a strong cultural appreciation for Hispanic origin and desire to hire a native, fluent, Spanish-speaking applicant from a Spanish country. It is generally unacceptable to have a requirement that the person be born in a Spanish country or his or her native language is Spanish. The essential question is "Can the applicant do the essential functions of the job?" and the applicant's birthplace probably doesn't matter.

Questions regarding marital status and gender are generally inappropriate unless relevant to the job. If an organization is hiring a director of a Jewish women's organization, then it may be appropriate to seek a female who is Jewish. On the other hand, it is generally inappropriate to ask questions to an applicant about sex, marital status, number and ages of children or dependents, obligations for childcare, pregnancy, or child bearing or birth control, which are irrelevant to performing the essential functions of the job.

Another area that has been somewhat contentious in school districts involves an applicant's race, color, and ethnicity. Generally using these factors as a basis for hiring decisions is illegal but may be appropriate in special situations in meeting the affirmative action requirements or when an organization *Note* has established a *bona fide occupational qualification* (BFOQ). An example of a BFOQ is a situation where a religious institution needs to hire a person of a specific religion to satisfy the job requirements. Also in some cases, a school district that has a student body that is 100 percent African American might seek an African-American candidate for the principal of the school. The school district may establish that race in this situation is an essential function to support the needs of the organization. Cases like this may involve potential for reverse discrimination. There have been many cases throughout history in the United States where reverse discrimination has been charged. Given the myriad of affirmative action programs and evolving legislation, it is not always clear cut, and legal counsel should be obtained.

Another controversial area in hiring involves the disability of an applicant. The Americans with Disabilities Act (ADA) of 1990 prohibits employment discrimination against people with physical or mental disabilities who can perform the essential functions of the job with or without reasonable accommodations. Therefore, during an interview, it is generally unacceptable to ask the applicant questions regarding his or her general medical condition, state of health, or other physical or mental disabilities. It is also generally unacceptable to ask whether an applicant has filed past worker's compensation claims. These questions may reveal medical information that could be used to discriminate against the applicant. A common question that can be asked by interviewers is "Can you perform the essential functions of the job you are applying for with or without reasonable accommodation?" This question gets to the heart of whether an applicant can perform the basic job, which should be the fundamental objective of the interview. Determining the definition of reasonable accommodation can be unclear. Various legal experts have tried to define this term by using past case law (Anyaso, 2008). For example, it may be entirely appropriate and expected to spend a few hundred dollars to provide a ramp for wheelchair employee or special ergonomic support devices or cushions that can assist a disabled person in performing the essential functions of a job. However, it may be an undue burden to require a school board to destroy an entire building and rebuild it with an expensive elevator

BFOQ bona fide occupational qualification

to accommodate a disabled individual. Again, these are questions that school administrators need to consult with local legal counsel.

Another controversial area that has emerged in recent times is religious affiliation and ability to work during school hours. It is acceptable to ask an applicant if he or she is able to perform the essential functions of the job and work hours. However, questions regarding the applicant's religion and observation of religious days are generally unacceptable. This situation may pose controversy later if the employee's religious days fall on regular school days and the employee requests an extended leave of absence. Generally there are contractual personal leave days that can be used. However, this issue may be more problematic when an extended leave is desired.

Other questions regarding military service, organizational activities, and emergency notification need to be legally followed as well. Any questions that reveal a person's race, religious creed, color, national origin, ancestry, sex, or age that may be disclosed by answering these questions are generally unacceptable. However, asking an applicant to list all organizations or special military experience that are relevant to the job is generally appropriate. Further information on these laws can be obtained from the EEOC.

Steps in Conducting the Interview Session

1. Interview Preparation
   - Review questions (classified and nonclassified)
   - Review pre-employment legal guidelines
   - Review and make copies of candidate's resume
   - Make copies of district benefits *brochure*
   - Obtain copy of district materials (e.g., school improvement plan, community, housing, etc.)
   - Make copy of organizational chart
2. Opening/Icebreaker (small talk, offer drink, obey legal guidelines)
3. Data Check (confirm candidate and correct position)
4. School District Overview (brief review of the school organization)
5. Candidate Questions (use prepared standard questions)
6. Candidate Needs
   - Candidate questions about job
   - Ask what candidate desires in job or career
7. Promote the District (benefits, community, etc.)

8. Ask If Candidate Has Any Questions
9. Close the Session
   - Ask permission for reference check
   - Ask and obtain signature for background check
   - Ask permission and set up drug test
   - Explain next steps
   - Give tour of district or school
10. Post-Session and Follow-up Items
    - Debrief session with interviewing team
    - Make hiring decision
    - Document decisions and information
    - Check references
    - Conduct background check
    - Schedule drug test
    - Complete employment form
    - Prepare follow-up letter (next step or rejection letter)

Once the search committee has been well trained in pre-employment laws, they need to prepare for conducting interview. See "Steps in Conducting the Interview Session." During the interview preparation phase, the screening committee members should understand as much as they can about the school district. Applicants will undoubtedly have questions about the school district that will need to be answered. Some of these questions may relate to the union contract, human resource manual, benefits, community and business affiliation, housing availability, and so on. It is often good to prepare a copy of the organizational chart so that applicants can develop a clear understanding of the people and functions within the organization.

During the actual interview session, it is important to start out with an icebreaker to make the applicant feel comfortable and to humanize the session. Questions about the traffic or weather are fairly innocuous and can be good icebreakers. The first formal questions are called *data check questions*, which are questions that confirm the applicant's name, the position being applied for, and start date. It is not unusual during an interview to find that the wrong applicant is applying for the wrong job at the wrong time, and starting out with a data check can help resolve these issues and prevent wasted time and further embarrassment to all parties.

Once the interview session begins, it is appropriate to start by introducing all the members of the committee and providing an overview of the school district. The interviewers then generally begin asking the applicant the formally prepared questions (Perlmutter, 2011). Some typical interview questions include:

1. Describe your leadership style.
2. Describe your teaching style.
3. Describe your teaching philosophy.
4. List examples of professional skill development you have taken in the past five years.
5. Give us an example of how you have handled a difficult student disciplinary problem.
6. What are your greatest strengths?
7. What are your greatest weaknesses?
8. Describe your decision-making process in solving complex educational issues.

Many of the questions that are prepared relate to categories such as instruction, curriculum, discipline, education, experience, interpersonal skills, and teaching style. Questions should be designed that allow the screening committee to obtain applicant information on how well the applicant can perform the essential functions of the job. During the interview session, the members should pay close attention to the answers, document responses, and exhibit proper listening skills (Jenkins, 2010). Some examples include:

- Avoid overreacting to an applicant's statement.
- Avoid irritating distractions, such as excessive writing, that may distract the applicant.
- Maintain good eye contact.
- Demonstrate proper expressions and acknowledgment of applicant's statements.
- Avoid prejudging the applicant or establishing a positive or negative "halo" effect.
- Use effective nonverbal behaviors.
- Paraphrase the applicant's statements to gain assurance of understanding.
- Thank the applicant for their comments and questions.

A part of the interview session should allow the applicant to ask questions about the job and school district. Also it is often beneficial to provide a tour of the facilities and to promote the school district and community. This helps sell the school and establish good public relations even if the applicant does not take the job.

The closing of the interview session should not be abrupt and should conclude in a professional manner. Typical actions include asking for permission for reference checks, obtaining a signature for a background check, permission to schedule a drug test or medical physical, and an explanation of the next steps in the process. It is important during the closing that the members refrain from giving applicants an impression that they will receive a job offer. It is generally acceptable to inform the applicants that, once all candidates have been interviewed and a decision has been made, they will be contacted.

After the interview session has concluded, much of the work begins with the post-session follow-up. This session is critical for the screening committee members to thoroughly evaluate the applicant and make decisions for the next steps. Exhibit 2.3 provides a sample of a typical interview evaluation form. There are many types of evaluation forms that can be used to assess an applicant after an interview. Every school district should develop a form that is best for the organization and is legally compliant. It is generally advisable to meet as soon as possible after an interview to capture everyone's impressions and review comments.

Some typical categories to evaluate include education knowledge, experience, interpersonal communication, and technology. The decision whether to extend an offer to a candidate can also be made. Also comments justifying a member's rating decision should be documented. When completed, all interview evaluation forms should be collected, filed, and kept for future use should there be an audit or discrimination claim.

After completing reference checks and documenting all information, the background check and drug and medical exams often occur. The candidate is generally extended an offer for employment and signs a release form (permission to conduct the background check) prior to completion of medical exams or background checks. The school district also needs to obtain official transcripts and other certifications or licenses.

There are many types of investigations that can be conducted for the background check. The investigation is performed by an outside agency and includes a search of public records on criminal convictions, incidents of dishonesty, moral turpitude, violence, drug-related offenses, credit bureau

Name of Applicant:			Interview Date:		
Position:			Lead Interviewer:		
Please complete the questions below after interviewing the applicant.					
	Unable to evaluate	Below average	Average	Above average	Excellent
EDUCATION (general background and knowledge)	0	1	2	3	4
EXPERIENCE (practical teaching experience)	0	1	2	3	4
INTERPERSONAL SKILLS (ability to relate to people)	0	1	2	3	4
COMMUNICATION SKILLS (verbal, non-verbal and written skills)	0	1	2	3	4
TECHOLOGY SKILLS (proficiency in using technology)	0	1	2	3	4
				TOTAL SCORE	_____
Rating Recommendation (circle one)	Hire		Consider	Do not hire	
Comments					
Interview Team: 1.					
2.					
3.					

EXHIBIT 2.3
Example of Interview Evaluation Form

information, history of driving infractions or accidents, previous employment records, and other possible public and proprietary records. A written request is generally obtained within sixty days of any adverse action or decision, although these time periods may vary from school district to school district and investigative agency. Other typical information included in an investigation is the applicant's full legal name, addresses within the last five to ten years, previous names or aliases, social security number, date of birth, driver's license number and state, and a complete signature and authorization date.

There are many guidelines when conducting *background checks*, and employers must abide by federal and state laws to avoid harm to applicants and lawsuits. Investigations that have no apparent connection to the job should be avoided. Many states have *fair credit reporting acts* and standards for conducting employment background checks that need to be followed. For example, the State of California provides a summary of the state's Fair

Credit Reporting Act (FCRA) to all persons that outlines their rights under the FCRA and what to do when their rights have been violated. According to the FCRA, when an outside agency prepares an investigative report, an applicant has a right to have notice if neighbors, friends, or associates have been interviewed regarding his or her character, general reputation, personal characteristics, or mode of living. Generally, there are statutes of limitations as well. For example, negative information may not be reported after seven years. However, exceptions are often made for bankruptcy and criminal convictions relevant to the job. Generally employers need to give an applicant a *pre-adverse action notice* with the background report if an adverse action has been taken (Fair Credit Reporting Act, State of California, 2012). In addition, federal law provides FCRA and publications that can assist both employers and applicants in following the fair credit standards and practices. Generally, all applicants have the right to know the extent of a background check and how it will be used for screening purposes. Applicants have rights, and permission must be obtained by the prospective employee.

Employers are subject to monetary penalties if applicants' rights are violated. However, some states may not require an employer to give an applicant a copy of the background check other than information obtained through public records. Examples of non-public-record information include verification and information from past employers, information from individuals providing references, and third-party investigation data.

Some employers include a self-screening section that allows applicants to obtain a copy of public record information and to waive their rights for a copy of this information. If applicants do not waive their rights to receive a copy of public information, they have approximately one week to obtain receipt. Also it is not uncommon that public records may contain inaccurate information about people. Generally an applicant can dispute in writing to the school district any inaccurate information obtained in the investigative public record report. The applicant may need to obtain legal counsel to clarify discrepancies and correct the public record. Examples of inaccurate or outdated information may pertain to court records for criminal activity that have been expunged by the applicant. Each state also has different laws regarding information about arrests, indictments, and misdemeanor complaints. For example, the State of California allows any indictments and related matters that have not come to trial or have been resolved to be reported on a background check report (Fair Credit Reporting Act, State of California, 2012).

There are also statutes of limitations on obtaining information on criminal convictions, arrests, and indictments. If a full pardon has been granted by law, then convictions cannot be on a report. There are many agencies that provide background check services with varying degrees of capabilities. Most agencies investigate public record databases, although there are more extensive private and federal databases. For example, the Federal Bureau of Investigation (FBI) has a database called the National Crime Information Center (NCIC) that can in some cases be accessed in cooperation with the agency (National Crime Information Center, 2012). Generally, the FBI will need to know the type of job position and concern prior to cooperating or giving permission to use the database.

A school board must perform due diligence, especially in verifying education, certification, and criminal and sex offender background checks to ensure the protection of students. Exhibit 2.4 shows examples of a pre-employment screening search for an applicant background check. This is a competitive business, and there are many different prices depending upon the extent of the screening services desired. Typical screening areas are social security verification, credit history reports, driver's license search, county criminal records searches, federal criminal records, employment verification, sex offender registry reports, and education and certification verification.

Another controversial issue that can arise during the screening process is the requirement of a *polygraph examination.* Organizations in general cannot require a job applicant to take an employment polygraph test. This requirement can only be done once the specific conditions are met that involve a good-faith effort by the employer to ensure the safety and security of people within an organization. This situation might include certain security or safety personnel of a school district that has a significant impact on the health and safety of the students and staff. Additional information on the use of polygraphs can be obtained through the American Polygraph Association and state and federal Department of Labor regulations.

The use of psychological and behavioral tests and assessment centers has been controversial in the selection process. Generally these assessments have been reserved for administrative and specialized positions. For example, data processors may be required to demonstrate keyboarding proficiency, or security people may need to pass a safety procedures examination. An administrator might be required to complete an *in-basket exercise* to demonstrate leadership and management decision-making proficiency. Sometimes assessment centers are used to screen candidates for a position through use of trained profession-

Search	Description
Social Security Verification	Verifies a valid social security number or use of multiple numbers or aliases
Driver's License	Verifies a driver's license, specific type, issue date, and restrictions
Credit History	Searches credit bureau reports on applicant's financial activities
County Civil Record	Reviews all county civil litigation records available in the county courthouse
County Criminal Record	Examines all criminal activity contained in the clerk of court's office as generally matched by name, date of birth, social security number, and address
Federal Criminal Record	Examines U.S. federal district courthouse databases for records of crimes and violations of federal law
Employment Verification	Seeks details on dates of employment, position, and job-related information of previous employment history
Education Verification	Searches and verifies education experience degrees, institutions, date of attendance, and degrees obtained
State Certifications and Licenses	Verifies Department of Education applicant's certification and licenses
Sex Offender Registry Search	Examines all registered sex offenders and applicant's current and former residences

EXHIBIT 2.4
Examples of Applicant Background Checks

als. Discretion should be used when using assessment centers to ensure that there is adequate *construct validity* and a relationship between these assessment activities and the essential job functions. Caution should also be given when using personality tests to assess an applicant. There are numerous personality tests that have evolved from the personality styles articulated by Carl Jung's four styles of the Thinker, Doer, Feeler, and Intuitor (Jung, 1923). While assessing the personality style of an applicant may be interesting and somewhat useful in comparing existing team members' styles with an applicant, these tests should not be used as a sole reason for hiring a person. Also, the construct validity of these tests may be questionable given that people may demonstrate different styles depending upon the situation he or she is placed in. For example, while working under pleasant conditions, an employee may demonstrate one style, but under stressful conditions, another style may be exhibited.

One of the difficult aspects in evaluating an applicant for a position involves making a determination whether there is a good fit between the

Construct Validity

applicant and the school. The search committee members should be aware of the myriad of applicant danger signs in hiring a person. Some of these are:

- Frequent and short employment,
- Employment history discrepancies,
- Actual job duty discrepancies,
- Applicant refuses to consent to background check or references,
- False application or false submission of employment data,
- Extensive negative comments toward past employers, and
- Unclear or confusing reasons for leaving past employers.

However, caution should be exercised when attempting to prejudge an applicant solely based upon these danger signs. For example, in the past, a frequent danger sign was the short duration of employment by a candidate. This is known as *job hopping* and might send a signal to a prospective employer that an applicant may not be a long-term employee. However, within the past couple decades, the frequent changing of jobs has been more common among employees due to the economy. Therefore, less credence might be placed on applicants who change jobs frequently. Applicants who have gained a variety of experiences from different school districts may offer valuable knowledge and skills for a school district, especially at the administrative level.

Considerable legislative and legal attention has been given to federal and state laws concerning the recruiting, screening, interviewing, and hiring of applicants. Courts have tended to place the burden of proof on the school district rather than the applicant when determining whether discrimination has taken place (Actkinson, 2011). The school district needs to provide evidence that there has been no discrimination of, disparate treatment of, or adverse impact on applicants during this selection process. Federal law does provide protection for employers to allow legal discrimination when there is evidence of a BFOQ.

A BFOQ can be established when a school district demonstrates operational necessity for discriminating against a protected class or favors one person over another. For example, an institution that has a religious affiliation and requires that all employees be of a specific religious faith may constitute a BFOQ defense. The BFOQ defense is generally more applicable to private schools than public schools. However a public school might employ a BFOQ defense when the safety or health of students or employees is impacted. For example, a school district may impose a mandatory age requirement for bus drivers or in supervising students. If a lawsuit arises for a BFOQ, it can be costly and time consuming for the school district. Past case law may help determine the legitimacy of a BFOQ, but ultimately the court will render the final decision.

The selection of the best candidate should be based upon the job description, needs of the organization, and legal compliance. The search committee members can use a spreadsheet listing the applicants' names in rank order and matched against the selection criteria. This information can be examined with the interview evaluation, applicant credentials, transcripts, references, and background check in making a selection decision. The final decision to extend an offer of employment should be approved by the superintendent and/or school board. An important step in this process is to notify the applicants who have been selected for positions with a formal letter. The offer for employment is often contingent upon satisfactory completion of all background checks and medical examination.

It is also common courtesy to send a letter to the applicants who have been rejected. Should the top selected candidate reject the offer, other candidates would then be considered. Also, when committee members talk to applicants who have been rejected, it is critical that this discussion be undertaken in a professional manner and follow guidelines, such as:

1. Be direct but personal.
2. Do not become defensive about the decision.
3. Do not make future promises or try to appease the applicant.
4. Be professional and courteous.
5. Document the discussion.
6. Do not become overly positive or give indications for future employment opportunities.
7. Do not disclose personal or investigation report information that should remain confidential.

The final completion of the interview and selection process concludes with documenting all information, filing the information, notifying all internal staff members, and making arrangements for the candidate's employment.

ORIENTATING NEW EMPLOYEES
Once a candidate has been employed, the next step is to conduct a proper orientation and indoctrination program (Haggarty, 2011). This is especially

important for new teachers and staff members entering the education institution for the first time. This program should provide an opportunity to clarify job responsibilities and expectations, understand the history of the school district, meet fellow teachers and staff members, understand policies and procedures, and become comfortable with the new work environment. "New Employee Orientation Information" lists some of the typical employee orientation information covered for new employees.

<u>New Employee Orientation Information</u>
1. District Strategic Plan
2. Vision and Mission Statements of the School
3. School Improvement Plan (SIP)
4. District Policies and Procedures
5. Solving Difficulties, Problems, and Complaints
6. Hours of Work
7. Performance Reviews and Evaluations
8. Infectious Disease Policies
9. Employee Conduct and Corrective Action
10. Substance Abuse Policy and Dress Code
11. Benefits, Staff Development, Holidays, and Employee Purchase and Services
12. Compensation, Pay Procedures, and Time Records
13. Leave of Absences: Personal, Medical, and Family Leave
14. Work Areas: Building Evacuation and Fire Alarm, Parking, Safety, and Security
15. Technology and Software
16. Union Contract and Regulations

Many human resource manuals stipulate that organizations subscribe to an *employee at will* policy, which implies that employees are free to resign at any time without reason and likewise the organization has the right to terminate an employee's employment at any time with or without reason or notice. However, for employees who belong to a union, the contractual agreements would stipulate conditions for employment. Also, while many private and charter schools may not have union contracts or employment agreements, federal and state laws would still apply. New employee processing often involves the employees obtaining necessary supplies and equipment to perform their work. Typical items often included are employee badges, key cards, photo identification badge, timekeeping information, technology equipment, computer user ID and password, and work supplies.

New employees also have certain rights to human resource records and information as granted by federal and state laws (U.S. Equal Employment Opportunity Commission, 2011). For example, employees may have the right to review their file and to obtain a copy. Some information may be restricted, such as letters of reference and administrative planning information if the disclosure would constitute an unwarranted invasion of personal privacy. Also employees may have access to medical examination for conditions that do not pose a health or safety danger to others. Generally, new employees need to obtain a medical examination and be free from infectious diseases that can harm others. In addition, many organizations have nonsolicitation and distribution activities during work time and dress codes. Other areas to be covered include parking arrangements, safety, security, computer software and supplies, use of copy machine, emergency evacuation procedures, and office management protocol in handling outside visitors. Other topics for new teachers include an overview of district teaching policies and procedures, blood-borne pathogens and infectious disease, curriculum and instruction expectations, and the teaching evaluation process.

A proper staff induction program is especially important for new teachers. Research has shown that up to one third of new teachers leave a school district within three years (National Center for Education Statistics, 2012). There are several reasons for teacher attrition, such as high expectations by administrators, long hours working on lesson plans, grading, and handling student and parent issues. Therefore, providing meaningful new teacher orientation and mentoring programs can help support new teachers and reduce attrition (Simon, 2011).

New teacher induction generally begins with completing all the necessary federal and state employment forms. For example, the I-9 Employment Eligibility Verification Form is required by the Department of Homeland Security for all employees in the United States. The purpose of this form is to document all new employees whether they are a citizen of the United States or not. This requirement became effective in November 1986 and requires information on citizenship and eligibility of people for employment in the United States. Employers are responsible for verifying employment authorization status and are required to obtain acceptable documents, such as a U.S. passport, foreign passport, temporary immigrant visa, driver's license or identification card issued by a state within the United States that contains a photograph, voter's registration card, military card, social security card, or birth certificate.

There are some exceptions to these requirements, such as nonimmigrant aliens who are authorized to work in the country can show a foreign passport or other endorsements of the alien's nonimmigrant status. In cases where an employee is under the age of eighteen, documents that are permissible include a school record or report card, physician or hospital record, and day-care or nursery record. In some cases a taxpayer identification number and certification may be required.

SUMMARY

The recruiting of applicants and orientation of employees requires a systematic and comprehensive knowledge in recruiting, selecting, orientation, and indoctrination. The overall purpose is to select the best candidates for a position and provide the proper orientation, mentoring, and professional development that support the employee's success within the organization. Moreover, incorporating an effective orientation program can help ensure that employees perform to the standards required by the organization and allow the school district to remain legally compliant.

There are numerous resources available to assist educators in this entire process and should be utilized to develop the best systems and processes that are relevant for an organization. Moreover, developing a collaborative approach with involvement by all stakeholders can help to ensure agreement and success to the recruiting and professional development programs.

CASE STUDY

You have been recently hired as the school principal for Edwards High School in the southeastern United States. The school has approximately 1,200 students and a teaching faculty who are mainly white, middle-aged men. The academic performance of the students is average as compared to other school districts in the state. There has not been much involvement of the parents or community within the school. Due to budgetary constraints, class size has been high, with most classes containing thirty-five to forty students.

Also, there is a need for replacing several teachers who will be retiring at the end of the school year as well as several classified staff. Some of the facilities are old and need to be replaced, such as student wheelchair ramps, broken windows, and collapsed fences along the school grounds. The superintendent has also mentioned to you that the performance evaluation system is outdated and that some local area school districts have been using a new computerized appraisal system. He also mentioned that Edwards High School has never had a mentoring program since they have not needed to hire new employees for several years. Overall, the school board and superintendent have high hopes for you as a new principal.

The school board and superintendent have charged you, as the new principal, to submit six goals for the high school for the ensuing school year. Based upon the information in this case, please develop six goals, and list them in priority order.

EXERCISES AND DISCUSSION QUESTIONS

1. List the steps and characteristics for developing a comprehensive recruiting program at a school.
2. List and describe some of the relevant federal, state, and school laws and policies impacting the selection process.
3. List the characteristics of an effective new teacher orientation program.
4. Outline the types of topics for a typical new employee orientation program.
5. List the five categories and examples for a professional development program.
6. Describe some major reasons for establishing a new employee orientation program.
7. Describe some of the typical problems in interviewing applicants for a position.
8. List and describe some of the pertinent federal and state EEOC laws when orientating a new employee to the job.
9. Describe how to keep all employees informed about who are new employees in a school district.
10. List and describe several questions when interviewing an applicant for a teacher position.

REFERENCES

Actkinson, J. (2011). Solid interview skills: Your journey to a job offer. *School Library Journal, 57* (4), 56–57.

Anyaso, H. (2008). Approaching diversity from the top down. *Diverse: Issues in Higher Education, 25* (18), 20–21.

Balter, D., & Duncombe, W. (2008). Recruiting highly qualified teachers: Do district recruitment practices matter? *Public Finance Review, 36*(1), 33–62.

Bilimoria, D. (2010). The search is on: Engendering faculty diversity through more effective search and recruitment. *Change, 42* (4), 27–32.

Fair Credit Reporting Act, State of California: www2.courtinfo.ca.gov/protem/ courses/sm_claims/benchbk/5_52-5_59.pdf.

Haggarty, L. (2011). Improving the learning of newly qualified teachers in the induction year. *British Educational Research Journal, 37* (6), 935–54.

Herreid, C. (2010). How to survive an academic job interview. *Journal of College Science Teaching, 39* (3), 10–15.

Jenkins, R. (2010). How to stand out in your interview. *Chronicle of Higher Education, 56* (23), A38–A39.

Jung, C. (1923). *Psychological types.* New York: Harmony Books.

Kollie, E. (2008). As the baby boomers retire: Preparing to fill the open positions. *School Planning & Management, 47* (10), 22–24.

Mason, R. (2010). Principal hiring practices: Toward a reduction of uncertainty. *Clearing House, 83* (5), 186–93.

National Center for Education Statistics (2012): http://nces.ed.gov/2012.

National Crime Information Center: www.fas.org/irp/agency/doj/fbi/is/ncic.htm.

Odden, A. (2011). Manage human capital strategically. *Phi Delta Kappan, 92* (7), 8–12.

Perlmutter, D. (2011). How to play left field at job interviews. *Chronicle of Higher Education.* http://chronicle.com/article/How-to-Play-Left-Field-at-Job/129118.

Simon, S. (2011). Characteristics of effective professional development for early career science teachers. *Research in Science & Technological Education, 29* (1), 5–23.

U.S. Equal Employment Opportunity Commission. (2011). Laws and guidance. www.eeoc.gov/laws.

3

Mentoring and Professional Development

OBJECTIVES

At the conclusion of this chapter, you will be able to:

1. Understand new employee mentoring procedures used by school leaders (ELCC 3.1; ISLLC 3).
2. Differentiate between federal and state laws that impact employee evaluation practices (ELCC 6.1, 6.2, 6.3; ISLLC 6).
3. Understand methods of professional development (ELCC 3.1; ISLLC 3).
4. Describe different types of performance appraisal forms (ELCC 3.1, 3.3; ISLLC 3).
5. Understand different strategies in conducting performance evaluations (ELCC 2.1, 3.3; ISLLC 3).
6. Describe the process of appraising employees' performance (ELCC 3.3, 6.1; ISLLC 3, 6).

MENTORING EMPLOYEES

One of the most effective strategies that can support a new teacher is a mentoring program (Hanson, 2010). Assigning an experienced teacher who can act as a mentor for the new teacher on matters such as dealing with disruptive students, personal issues, and administrative requirements can help contribute to successful employment. The mentor can also help orientate the new teacher to the school and provide effective coaching on the new teacher's performance. The selection of dedicated, committed, credible, and experienced teachers are generally prerequisites for teacher mentors. In addition all teacher mentors should be well trained in how to be an effective coach. Topics might include understanding instruction and curriculum, managing student discipline, understanding the school district operations, and district policies and procedures. In addition to these professional qualities, an effective mentor needs effective coaching qualities, which include being sensitive, a good listener, empathetic, accessible, supportive, honest, and trustworthy.

While there may be added costs to the school district for these programs, the time and money that can be saved by not needing to conduct a search to replace teachers can well justify the program. Some benefits for the teacher mentor include additional compensation, release time, satisfaction of helping others, and support for the school district. A good mentoring program should be designed to allow for regular observations of the new teacher, time for providing coaching, and time for following up on performance issues. Mentors should also, in turn, be evaluated by administrators to ensure their performance is acceptable. Exhibit 3.1 lists typical information for a teacher mentoring program.

When working with a new teacher, the mentor should begin by establishing rapport. He or she should cover the basics teaching responsibilities, lesson

Content	Description
School Facilities and Equipment	Orientation and location of media equipment, technology, supplies, special services, teacher parking, etc.
School Procedures	Hours of work, attendance, policies, dress code, crisis management, testing policies, student emergencies, etc.
Resource Access	Use of discretionary funds, shared equipment and materials, textbooks, supplemental materials, classroom teaching supplies, requisitions, etc.
Curriculum and Instruction	Lesson plan procedures and expectations, subject matter experts, grading procedures, school calendar and schedule, curriculum mapping, district office expectations, and location of guide manuals
Student Discipline Management	Student discipline procedures and expectations, how to handle disciplinary offenses, initiating a parent conference, the referral process, etc.

EXHIBIT 3.1
Examples of Information in a Mentor Program

plan preparation, strategies in beginning a class, completing student absentee records, and classroom management. Other items might include dealing with student academic problems, responding to a fire or disaster drill, writing a syllabus and course outline, and dealing with parent issues.

One of the most important topics to cover with a new teacher is time management. The new teacher needs to become proficient in multitasking skills. Some of the common time wasters for a new teacher include telephone interruptions, inadequate planning, oversocializing, meetings, procrastinating, dealing with confusing responsibilities or expectations, poor communications, and personal disorganization. A good mentor should coach the new teacher on these time wasters and offer strategies for overcoming them, which might include listing goals for each day, preparing work in advance, making a daily to-do list, eliminating unproductive activities, and setting deadlines for accomplishing work tasks.

The mentor should make regular observations of the new teacher's instruction and provide feedback. The basic steps for conducting a teacher observation include preconference, observation, analysis, and post-conference feedback. During the preconference discussion, the mentor schedules the time and place for observation in collaboration with the new teacher. During the observation, the mentor should record and evaluate the new teacher on all aspects of teaching and classroom management. Afterward, a careful analysis and review of the information should be completed in preparation for the post-conference meeting. During this meeting, the mentor should give constructive feedback to the new teacher. At times the mentor may need to provide on-the-job training for the new teacher, which includes five basic steps as outlined in exhibit 3.2.

The mentor should regularly provide casual feedback by asking questions, such as "Describe things that are going well for you," "Describe some areas that you would like to improve," "What can I do as a mentor to better assist you?" The feedback given to new teachers by the mentor should be done on a formative versus summative basis. Formative feedback is an ongoing review designed to give informal assessment without the formal supervisory evaluation that becomes part of the new teacher's performance record. This process allows the new teacher to freely ask questions and to improve performance without the worry of the feedback being used against him or her. Summative feedback is conducted generally by the new teacher's supervisor and is used

Steps (5 Ps)	Description
Plan	Make preparations for the on-the-job demonstration.
Present	Demonstrate the behavior (instruction or handling of a discipline problem).
Create a Positive Environment	Establish a good rapport and give a constructive, positive atmosphere for the teacher.
Perform the Behavior	The new teacher performs the behavior while the mentor observes.
Performance Evaluation	The mentor gives immediate performance feedback and follows up with the new teacher.

EXHIBIT 3.2
The Five Steps of On-the-Job Mentor Training

as a formal and official record of performance. See "Steps in Conducting a Formative Employee Coaching Session."

Steps in Conducting a Formative Employee Coaching Session
1. Describe the performance.
2. State expectations or standards.
3. Ask new teacher for reflection.
4. Listen, empathize, and paraphrase.
5. Collaboratively identify root cause.
6. Ask for suggestions on actions to improve.
7. Discuss and agree upon actions.
8. Thank the new teacher, and build his or her confidence.

During the first step of the formative coaching session, the mentor should *describe the performance* of the new teacher. During this stage, the mentor begins by humanizing the setting and being objective but direct in describing performance that needs to be improved. For example, issues might include the need for improved instruction, handling of a student disciplinary case, or improving lesson plans. Step 2 requires the mentor to describe the *desired expectation* or standard. For example, the mentor may state that lesson plans need to be error free, well organized, and contain all components outlined in the school policy manual.

Step 3 involves the new teacher *reflecting upon his or her performance* and identifying positive behaviors and areas in need of improvement. This reflection can be a valuable method to help a new teacher examine his or her performance without the mentor directly stating the problem. For example, the new teacher may conclude that he or she is having difficulty handling student misbehavior and needs to more thoroughly understand and administer the school district student disciplinary policies.

An important step in the formative coaching session is for the mentor to *sincerely listen*, empathize with his or her feelings, and paraphrase the new teacher's comments (step 4). The use of paraphrasing helps to verify what the new teacher stated and confirm mutual understanding. Typical statements might be "I can understand how you feel in a situation like this," "I can see how someone would have these feelings in a situation like this," or "I was once a new teacher as well and understand." Paraphrasing can also help to show that the mentor is demonstrating active listening and helps in personalizing the conversation and developing an atmosphere of respect.

Step 5 involves the new teacher collaboratively identifying the *root cause* of the performance problem. This step is similar to step 3 but goes into greater detail. For example, if a new teacher is experiencing difficulty in handling disciplinary problems, the potential root causes might include distractions from outside influences, health issues, a poor attitude, need for additional training, or a dysfunctional school environment. It is important for the mentor to reinforce the new teacher's responsibility for improvement and to provide encouragement for improvement.

The sixth step entails asking the new teacher for solutions for the performance issue. In this way the new teacher is more likely to accept the solution. It also allows the new teacher to take responsibility for his or her own behavior. For example, the new teacher may need to include more engaging instructional activities or learn to control his or her emotions when dealing with misbehavior.

In step 7, the mentor and new teacher should discuss and agree upon an action plan for resolving the performance issue. There may be some negotiation so they can collaboratively resolve the issue. The new teacher should propose a solution that is acceptable to the mentor since he or she will be more apt to accept the solution rather than it being imposed upon him or her. However, if the new teacher's suggestion is unacceptable to the mentor, further discussion may be necessary, and ultimately they will need to mutually arrive at an effective action. The last step, step 8, involves the mentor *thanking the new teacher* for participating in the coaching session and building his or her confidence. Building the confidence of a new teacher has reinforcing consequences.

Defense Mechanism	Description
Denial	Failing to accept responsibility for behavior
Projection	Believing the problem is someone else's, not the new teacher's
Reaction Formation	Reporting the same problem instead of correcting the behavior
Excessive Aggressiveness	Becoming hyperactive, difficulty focusing, and becoming easily distracted
Avoidance	Avoiding an issue rather than accepting responsibility
Defensiveness	Resisting acceptance of feedback
Rationalization	Justifying other reasons for his or her performance
Displacement	Taking out his or her frustrations on other people or the mentor

EXHIBIT 3.3
Typical Defense Mechanisms

Even if a mentor has difficulty in supporting a new teacher, especially for very poor performance incidents, the mentor needs to continue to maintain a positive working relationship, otherwise the mentor–new teacher relationship will be undermined. During the coaching process, the mentor should also be aware of his or her subtle, nonverbal cues that the new teacher may observe that are incongruent with the mentor's verbal message. The mentor may also suggest a follow-up session to review the new teacher's progress and/or additional measures.

When giving constructive feedback, a mentor needs to be aware of the typical *defense mechanisms* that are often displayed by new teachers (see exhibit 3.3). Defense mechanisms are those things that human beings do to protect themselves from experiencing bad feelings. New teachers can often feel vulnerable, especially if they experience several setbacks. Consequently, they may resort to defense mechanisms to prevent themselves from feeling bad. Understanding defense mechanisms can help a mentor in coaching the new teacher. New teachers may not resort to all of these defense mechanisms, but if the mentor sees patterns of one occurring, he or she can be in a better position to coach the new teacher.

PROFESSIONAL DEVELOPMENT

Every employee, regardless if he or she is a new teacher, should be involved in professional development. Professional development is an ongoing process and should be mutually designed by district administrators, department chairpersons, and teachers (Simon, 2011). See "Categories of Professional

Development." The selection of topics should be completed through collaboration with teachers and administrators in order to achieve mutual ownership (Bubb & Earley, 2009). There are five categories of professional development that can offer a viable approach to achieving quality programs.

Categories of Professional Development

1. **Teacher-Centered Development**
   - Managing Stress
   - Planning and Organizing   INTERNAL
   - Time Management
   - Handling Conflict
   - Values and Human Relations
   - Managing Diverse Students

2. **Classroom-Centered Development**
   - Managing Discipline
   - Improving Attendance
   - Classroom Management
   - Handling Complaints
   - Counseling Students
   - Managing Conflict

3. **School-Centered Development**
   - School Improvement Plan (SIP)
   - Problem Solving/Decision Making
   - Peer Mediation
   - Parent and Community Involvement —
   - Managing Charge and Conflict
   - Professional Learning Communities —

4. **Teaching-Centered Development**
   - Instructional Skills
   - Learning Styles
   - Curriculum Methods
   - Differentiated Instruction
   - Technology and Online Learning
   - Multiple Intelligences

5. **Student-Centered Development**
   - Building Self-Esteem
   - Individual Differences and Human Relations

- Motivation and Success
- Self-Management
- Test-Taking Skills
- Conflict Management

Teacher-Centered Development *Self-mgt*

While new teachers are often academically prepared for teaching, they sometimes lack essential skills of self-management. The ability to effectively meet administrative demands, handle school problems, solve day-to-day problems, and inspire students requires highly developed self-management skills. Some of these skills include managing strong emotions, planning and organizing, handling conflict, understanding personal value and human relations, interpersonal communications, leadership, and motivation. These topics can provide meaningful personal growth for new teachers as well as experienced teachers and help them become more effective in the classroom.

Classroom-Centered Development

Student discipline continues to be a major problem in our schools today (Simon, 2011). Learning new strategies to effectively handle student misbehavior is especially critical for new teachers. Other topics include classroom management, teaching challenging students, motivating students, improving attendance, managing conflict, handling complaints, counseling students, understanding legal issues involved in disciplining students, and classroom strategies. Developing skills in managing the classroom environment will directly contribute to students' achievement and quality of school life.

School-Centered Development

School-centered topics focus on developing new teacher skills that contribute directly to meeting school organizational needs. These areas include developing skills in parent–community relations, managing change, developing a school improvement plan (SIP), managing and coordinating educational resources, finances, teamwork, improving the school culture, and understanding professional learning communities. The educational leadership should include the entire staff in selecting the school-centered skills so everyone can create a collaborative approach in meeting school needs.

Teaching-Centered Development

Teaching-centered development is a fundamental requirement of all new and experienced teachers if they are to continue to make a difference in student learning. Some skill development areas include action research, instructional methodology, curriculum development, learning styles, multiple intelligences, multiculturalism, and strategies for student achievement. The field of education is rapidly changing, and the need to keep abreast of current instructional and curricular programs and technology is critical for all teachers.

Student-Centered Development

The last category focuses on student-centered activities that can directly help student performance and personal management. Topics include building self-esteem, understanding individual differences, values and human relations, personal motivation and success, test-taking skills, interpersonal relationships, study habits, handling stress, dealing with gangs and peer pressure, and making life choices. Helping teachers to learn to more effectively improve the skills students use to deal with individual problems can significantly contribute to developing their academic and personal growth.

School administrators can use a number of techniques to develop a *professional development program*, such as faculty surveys, staff focus groups, needs assessments, teacher interviews, and staff development committees. These methods can be beneficial in identifying the professional development needs of teachers and staff.

Administrators also need to understand that professional development is an ongoing process and should not expect instant miracles. The success of any professional development program is dependent upon the top administrators' support. School administrators should also celebrate achievements and recognize good performance of teachers who utilize the principles and strategies learned through these developmental programs.

Administrators can employ methods of professional development other than traditional workshops and seminars (Desimone, 2011). Examples of other methods include using the performance evaluation session as a way to improve teachers' performance, undertaking research and development projects, including new teachers in committees, staff meetings, field trips to other schools, participation in professional associations, team teaching, and providing professional development sessions during teacher in-service days.

PERFORMANCE EVALUATION

Performance evaluations are conducted at virtually all school districts. The state department of education, local school district policies, union contractual agreements, and federal programs such as the No Child Left Behind Act are some of the proponents of performance evaluations (Milanowski, 2011). Performance evaluations have increased in use because of the emphasis on performance accountability and standards. Using the performance evaluation process can be an important tool in helping to improve the performance of all teachers and staff within the school district (Sykes & Dibner, 2009).

Reasons for Conducting Performance Evaluations
1. Provide performance feedback
2. Help motivate people
3. Promote communications
4. Use as a basis for staff development
5. Validate and document performance
6. Document performance problems
7. Comply with legal mandates
8. Provide rewards for people
9. Maintain fairness and accountability

There are many reasons for conducting performance evaluations (see "Reasons for Conducting Performance Evaluations"). The performance evaluation should not be a single-purpose process whereby the supervisor quickly completes a form, holds a brief appraisal session, files the form, and then goes back to business as usual. The supervisor should not consider the performance evaluation as busy work or as a *compliance exercise* just to satisfy school district or legal requirements. This feeling by supervisors may exist when evaluating tenured faculty. Some supervisors may feel handicapped in evaluating low-performing, tenured teachers when union contractual obstacles make it difficult to terminate a tenured teacher. Supervisors should not take the easy way out and complete a quick or shallow performance review.

Performance evaluations can be a mechanism for accomplishing many goals. One reason for the evaluation is to give genuine constructive performance feedback to the employee, which can reinforce good performance and identify areas in need of improvement. The review session can also provide

salary/bonuses

an opportunity to motivate employees through intrinsic verbal praise and a basis for extrinsic rewards, such as salary increases and bonuses. The performance evaluation session can serve to help promote communications, review respective performance, and develop continuous improvement plans for the future. This communication can serve as a basis for further developing people by establishing goals and gaining input that can help the entire organization (Prather-Jones, 2011).

Another reason for conducting the performance evaluation session is to validate and document performance of employees. This documentation serves as a record for employee performance, which is needed when there is a need to terminate the employee in the future. Complying with legal and district policies is another reason to document performance problems. Lastly, the performance evaluation session can help to support personal accountability and provide a basis for financially rewarding employees. While many people experience some anxiety during the performance review session, the benefits generally outweigh the time and effort. The performance evaluation session can provide an opportunity for documenting the employee's performance and serve as a system of fairness by informing employees how well they are performing in the organization.

There are many types of performance evaluation systems, such as open narrative appraisals, formative and summative assessments, 360 performance evaluation, and rating systems. Some organizations utilize an *open narrative evaluation*, especially for high-level administrators and managers. In this system, the subordinate is asked to write a narrative regarding how well he or she performed during the year. This narrative is then used as a basis for a performance review session. This type of system is a more informal approach and is infrequently used.

The *formative assessment* is often used to support the summative evaluation process. During the formative assessment, informal feedback is given to the employee by the supervisor, and this information is not used as part of the employee's permanent evaluation record. The whole idea of formative assessment is to give informal feedback without the fear of the information negatively impacting the employee's performance. However, it is sometimes difficult to entirely disregard the information when preparing a summative report.

The *summative evaluation* is the most popular approach and consists of a combination rating assessment and narrative section on the evaluation form.

1206 Decatur St
20781

The evaluation forms can consist of a paper copy filed in a cabinet or an electronic copy stored on a computer.

The *360 performance evaluation* is a system that uses a multirater feedback process to obtain an evaluation on an employee. The feedback is generally provided by multiple supervisors, peers, support staff, community members, and possibly students. This system began during the 1950s in the corporate world and gradually gained popularity by human resources professionals. However, the system has been somewhat controversial in that it requires extensive time to collect the feedback, and some people feel that the information is not always accurate or used exclusively for developmental purposes. The 360 feedback may require gaining information from up to six to ten people. Each one of these individuals needs to complete an assessment of the employee. Sometimes the employee is allowed to choose the raters in addition to the supervisor. There are many decisions to be made in using a 360 approach, such as the selection of the type of feedback instrument, number of raters, how the raters are selected, the process to be used, degree of confidentiality, anonymity of the raters, and how to integrate the information into the performance management system. One advantage of the 360 process is that the employee receives multiple assessments. This may be more valuable than simply obtaining feedback from one supervisor. Also, when feedback is received from multiple stakeholders, a more diverse and comprehensive assessment can be obtained (Cleveland & Murphy, 1995).

The traditional *combination rating* and *open-comment evaluation* is still probably the most popular rating form (Milanowski, 2011). The evaluation of an employee is generally conducted on a semiannual or annual basis. Nontenured teachers are generally evaluated on a semiannual basis and tenured teachers evaluated annually. Conducting evaluations on a semiannual basis provides a good opportunity to obtain regular feedback, although this can be time consuming for both the employee and supervisor. Typically, the annual review is the requirement by school districts and state departments of education. Also the use of computer software has greatly increased the efficiency in completing and storing the evaluation forms into one database.

Regardless of the performance evaluation system used, there can be many problems associated with conducting the evaluation session (see "Problems in Conducting Performance Evaluations"). One problem is having sufficient time to prepare the form and complete the review session. The *leniency effect* occurs when a supervisor rates an employee too high in all the performance factors. This may happen when the supervisor desires to avoid dealing with potential employee dissatisfaction or resistance. The supervisor may also overrate an employee to avoid creating conflict with the employee. *Central tendency* occurs when the supervisor rates all the performance factors in the middle of the scale.

One of the most difficult aspects in completing performance evaluation is to ensure that all supervisors strive to have a common understanding of what constitutes the performance standards of an employee, a term called *inter-rater reliability*. It is generally advisable that all supervisors participate in performance evaluation training to understand the criteria for rating employees and different levels of *standards of performance.*

Problems in Conducting Performance Evaluations
1. Poor preparation and hasty review
2. Leniency effect
3. Central tendency rating
4. Recency effect rating
5. Poor inter-rater reliability
6. Personal prejudice and bias
7. Game playing
8. Rater indecisiveness
9. Being overly judgmental or emotional
10. Being overly confrontational and directive

Another problem with rating employees involves the human effect of harboring prejudice or bias toward an employee that may influence the rating. While the performance evaluation should be conducted objectively, it is nearly impossible to exclude personal subjectivity. *Game playing* is another problem with performance evaluations, which occurs when a supervisor over- or underrates an employee to support organizational politics. For example, if a new teacher is being rated during the first six months the, supervisor may rate the teacher lower to help protect himself or herself later should the supervisor desire to terminate the teacher for cause or deny the teacher tenure. The supervisor may also rate an employee lower in order to allow the employee room to grow. All these examples are game playing and should be avoided.

The supervisor should also avoid being too judgmental, emotional, directive, or controlling during the performance evaluation session. Other problems associated with conducting a performance evaluation include:

- Rating an employee based upon personal characteristics that violate discrimination laws,
- Telling the employee about the rating or performance of other employees in the organization,
- Changing a rating during the employee session because of undue pressure by the employee,
- Conducting the session in a nonprivate location,
- Focusing the appraisal review session on the supervisor's performance rather than largely on the employee,
- Giving false promises to an employee to avoid conflict with the employee,
- Rating the employee exceptionally high in an effort to gain the employee's favor and support, and
- Rating the employee low with the ulterior purpose of withholding a pay raise.

Most performance evaluation forms contain *performance rating levels* and *definitions*. For example, it is common to have a *five-level rating system* ranging from unacceptable to exceptional. Some forms have a three-rating level system consisting of not satisfactory, satisfactory, and outstanding. "Sample Performance Rating Levels and Definitions" shows a typical five-level performance rating with definitions. The rating levels should be explained to supervisors and employees so they have common understanding of standards of performance. There should be common agreement among supervisors regarding the general measures of performance. Supervisors should meet to review the overall percentages of the past ratings for each of the performance levels. For example, supervisors may feel that there are about 10 percent of employees who perform at the *exceptional* level, 45 percent who *exceed expectations*, 40 percent who *meet expectations*, 3 percent who *need improvement*, and only about 2 percent who are *unacceptable*. While these percentages should not be a requirement, the establishment of the percentages can help provide some general guidance and expectations for supervisor ratings. Establishing these general rating guidelines can also discourage *rating inflation* by supervisors.

SAMPLE PERFORMANCE RATING LEVELS AND DEFINITIONS

Exceptional

Employee's performance excels in all aspects of the job, having reached the ultimate in job performance on a sustained basis. Performance is a quality found only in a small percentage of people within the organization. Performance is recognizable as being consistently distinguished, which far exceeds all expectations of required job standards. Employee demonstrates a very high degree of expertise and serves as a model of excellence to other employees. This level of performance compares with the best the school has seen. Quality of work is superior.

Exceeds Expectations

Employee's performance clearly and consistently is beyond the criteria and standards required of a fully competent person at all times. Performance is beyond the level expected in fulfilling job requirements and achieving goals and objectives without any supervision. Employee demonstrates proficiency in performing the difficult and complex aspects of the job competently and thoroughly, including extra or unique tasks assigned, and often surpasses expectations. Quality of work is very good.

Meets Expectations

Employee's performance meets the criteria and standards of job performance for all aspects of the job. Performance is steady, reliable, and maintained with a minimum of supervision. Employee consistently demonstrates the expected standard of performance, which means accomplishing his or her goals and objectives, as well as generally meeting all required job standards. Quality of work is good.

Needs Improvement

Employee's performance usually meets the normal requirements in most of the job areas but occasionally fails to meet minimum criteria and standards of job performance. This rating would also apply to employees new to a position who are still learning all the aspects of the position. Performance at this level requires some improvement in order to meet or exceed the expectations of the job. Quality of work is inconsistent. This employee requires more than the normal guidance and direction.

Unacceptable

Employee's performance falls substantially short of the criteria and standard of job performance. Performance frequently fails to meet minimum requirements and objectives of almost all aspects of work. Employee demonstrates work clearly below the level of acceptability, and immediate and substantial improvement is necessary. Quality of work is poor. Significant improvement is needed.

The general performance factors contained in performance appraisal forms can vary dependent upon the type of position, such as exempt/classified employees (e.g., teachers, administrators, managers, assistant superintendents, superintendent) or nonexempt/nonclassified employees (e.g., custodians, support staff, administrative assistants, safety and security employees). Some performance evaluation forms contain more than one section of factors to be rated. For example, the first section might contain *job performance factors*, which are linked directly from the employee's job description. If there are too many responsibilities in the job description, they are often combined so that the total number of factors is about five or six. These factors are then rated using a standard scale directly related to specific job responsibilities of the employee.

The second section of the evaluation form often includes the *general performance factors*. Examples include quality and quantity of work, communication and interpersonal skills, dependability and reliability, ethics and service, collaboration, and safe work procedures. Some evaluation forms may have a third section containing *performance goals*. This section is often reserved for upper-level administrators. The premise of including a performance goals section is to support the achievement of the SIP initiatives and goals of the school district. In this case, administrators would write performance goals for the ensuing year that are approved by the board of education or supervisor. The idea of writing goals helps to document performance expectations, promote communications, and contribute to the overall employee's development.

The format for writing goals are often based on SMART criteria, which are *specific* (describe results to achieve), *measurable* (clearly written and state a level of achievement expected), *attainable* (are agreed upon by the supervisor and employee), *realistic* (are challenging, flexible, and achievable and provide stretch for the employee), and *timely* (are attainable within specified period of time). An example of a SMART goal might be "to increase the student achievement performance in the school by 10 percent as measured by the state standards-based achievement test by end of the school year." In addition to having professional SMART goals that are based on the operation of the school, it is common to have *personal development goals*, which are goals that help support the development of the employee. In essence there are two types of goals, *professional development*, which relate specifically to achieving the initiatives of the organization, and personal development goals, which help employee growth. See "Professional Development Goals" and "Personal Development Goals" for examples for an administrative position.

Professional Development Goals
1. Reduce student absenteeism by 10 percent by year end.
2. Improve test scores by 5 percent.
3. Develop a strategic community business program.
4. Develop a school crisis management program.
5. Purchase, install, and provide training for using SMART boards in technology classrooms.

Personal Development Goals
1. Improve writing skills.
2. Learn a new software program.
3. Improve time management skills.
4. Improve leadership skills.
5. Improve stress management

Each organization needs to design the performance evaluation system that is best for the organization. Fundamental questions for assessing the evaluation form include "Are the rating factors representative of the job position?" "Is the evaluation form comprehensive but easy to use?" "Is the content fair?" and "Do the employees like the form?" Also, whenever possible it is good to include standards by which each of the performance factors can be measured. The standards are' generally constructed as a rubric, which allows each of the levels to be distinguished in giving concrete examples of unsatisfactory, satisfactory, and superior performance. Exhibit 3.4 illustrates a typical performance appraisal rubric listing the standards of performance on a five-point scale. The use of performance appraisal rubrics can substantially improve inter-rater reliability and support objectivity and fairness.

Job Completion – Quality and quantity of work. Demonstrates accuracy, dependability, punctuality, thoroughness and timeliness of work in accordance with the job description.

_____ Exceptional: Known within the work unit and across divisions as a person who produces outstanding work. Consistently gets work done ahead of schedule. Adept at conversing with staff and administrators about best way to approach projects. Work is consistently of superior quality; errors are extremely rare. Performance has clearly demonstrated significant improvement in productivity and efficiency.

_____ Exceeds Expectations: Almost always completes assigned work on time or ahead of deadline. Work is virtually error-free. Rarely needs help or clarification from supervisor. Performance has contributed to fairly significant improvements in productivity and efficiency.

_____ Meets Expectations: Work is usually done on time; sometimes ahead of schedule. Errors are infrequent. Occasionally asks supervisor for help or clarification. Performance has contributed to improvements in productivity and efficiency.

_____ Needs Improvement: Assigned work is often not completed on time. Work often has errors or is incomplete. Supervisor needs to monitor regularly.

_____ Unacceptable: Assigned work is usually not done on time. Work is usually not complete or has errors. Needs close supervision.

Comments:

EXHIBIT 3.4
Performance Appraisal Rubric Listing Standards of Performance

"Steps in Conducting a Performance Evaluation Session" lists the typical steps for conducting the session. Every school district should provide sufficient training and guidelines in conducting the performance evaluation for all supervisors. The _preparation_ for the performance evaluation session should be thorough, step 1. It is important to schedule sufficient time and a location that is private and without distractions. Generally it is advisable for the employee to complete a self-assessment prior to the session. The employee can either send this self-assessment in advance to the supervisor or bring it to the evaluation session. The advantage of sending the self-assessment in advance allows the supervisor to anticipate the employee's evaluation, although it might bias the supervisor's own rating of the employee.

In step 2, the supervisor _introduces_ the session by providing an overview for the process, establishing expectations, defining criteria for ratings, and essentially setting the stage for the performance appraisal session. The third step involves the supervisor _reviewing_ all the performance ratings for all the sections on the form. Generally, a supervisor reviews each of the ratings and then gives an overall rating at the end, step 4. However, it is possible that the supervisor may want to give the overall rating prior to reviewing each of the rating sections. This might be the case when there is an outstanding employee and giving the overall rating in advance may help to reduce anxiety and allow for a more constructive discussion. When evaluating a poor performer, it is advisable to give the overall rating at the end so the supervisor can build justification for the rating, especially if the employee needs to be placed on probation.

After the rating has been given, it is often good to obtain the employee's *overall reaction* and then discuss general *development areas*, step 5. It is critical to *obtain the signature* of the employee on the performance appraisal form, step 6. The signature does not indicate that the employee agrees to the form but acknowledges that the form has been reviewed with the employee. Also, an optional step in the session might be for the supervisor to *discuss next year's goals* and agree upon the goals with the employee, step 7. In this case, the supervisor may request that the employee prepare in advance and bring these goals to the session. The performance appraisal session concludes by *documenting and filing all forms* in accordance with district policy, step 8. In the event that follow-up is needed for employees who may be placed on probation, then a schedule would be developed.

Steps in Conducting a Performance Evaluation Session
1. Prepare appraisal form (and schedule logistics for session).
2. Introduce session (set stage, criteria for ratings, and overview of process).
3. Review performance evaluation ratings (for each section of the form).
4. State the overall rating.
5. Obtain employee's reaction, and discuss developmental areas.
6. Obtain employee's signature on form.
7. Discuss and agree on next year's goals (optional).
8. Document and file performance evaluation form and information.

During the evaluation session, the supervisor should exhibit effective communication strategies, such as *anticipation*, *paraphrasing*, *silence*, and *limit-setting parameters*. For example, the use of anticipation is good when dealing with conflict during the session. If the supervisor anticipates that the employee may have a negative response, the supervisor may start by stating "I know that you have had difficulty with this performance issue in the past, however this is very important to me, and I don't mean to disrespect you. However, I would like to hear how you have improved in this area." By using anticipation strategy, the supervisor in essence anticipates an employee's potential reaction and tries to reduce the negative feelings that might occur. This can be an effective technique in building positive relationships during the session.

The use of paraphrasing is a common communication technique in which the supervisor simply puts in his or her own words what the employee is stating. For example, if the employee states that he or she is having difficulty with classroom management, the supervisor might put in his own words "So you feel you are having difficulty with controlling student misbehavior, and if so, I will be happy to work with you on this issue." In using this technique, the supervisor effectively paraphrases the employee's statements, reestablishes communication with the employee, and validates understanding of the performance issue.

Silence can be one of the most important communication strategies by the supervisor. Often there is a tendency for a supervisor to talk too much and not allow the employee to talk. The evaluation session should be a two-way communication and should allow sufficient time for the employee to provide comments. Never underestimate the power of allowing an employee to do the talking about his or her performance. Also, if the supervisor is slow to speak, the employee may be more inclined to talk and to express comments about his or her performance.

Another technique that can be useful is called *limit-setting parameters*. Essentially this technique provides limitations on the extent in which a supervisor can help support the performance of the employee, especially when the employee is asking for unrealistic support. The supervisor may respond by stating "I can do this, but I can't do that." This allows the supervisor to negotiate with the employee on support for correcting a performance issue. However, it should be emphasized that the accountability and responsibility for performance should ultimately be owned by the employee. However, limit-setting parameters are a good technique in introducing one's position and beginning the start of resolving performance discrepancies.

Critical to the performance appraisal session is adhering to federal, state, and school district laws and policies. There are several laws and potential union contract agreements that need to be understood by supervisors before administering the performance appraisal session. Some federal laws may include the Civil Rights Act of 1964, which prohibits discrimination on the basis of race, sex, religion, national origin, color, and certain medical conditions. The supervisor should make sure to restrain from noting any performance that references any of these factors that could be construed as discriminatory. For example, a supervisor should not rate a female employee lower just because she is pregnant.

Another law that may impact the appraisal is the Age Discrimination Act of 1967, which prohibits age discrimination beginning at forty. A supervisor should avoid comments such as "Nice job for an old man" or "You need to get with it and get out of the dark ages and learn technology like the young teachers." Comments like these are not only condescending but also may be legally unacceptable. Also, statements regarding people's lifestyle, if irrelevant to the employee's performance or employee codes of conduct, should be avoided.

Another law that may impact a performance appraisal session is the Americans with Disabilities Act of 1990, which prohibits discrimination on the basis of actual, previous, or perceived mental or physical disability. A supervisor should demonstrate caution in rating a disabled employee if reasonable accommodations have not been provided that could have improved his or her performance. The Title VII, Section 1604, Sexual Harassment Law may also apply during the performance appraisal session. A supervisor may genuinely express concern for an employee and may want to show support by giving the employee a hug or by embracing the employee. The supervisor should refrain from touching the employee in any manner other than perhaps a handshake. For example, upon conclusion of the performance appraisal session, the supervisor should refrain from tapping the employee on the shoulder as a sign of confidence or giving the employee a hug and stating "I have confidence in you. I know you'll do a great job." The sexual harassment law prohibits "any unwelcomed sexual advances or physical conduct of a sexual nature that unreasonably interferes with the individual's work performance or creates an intimidating, hostile or offensive working environment." While the supervisor may have good intentions, these types of actions may be construed to be sexual harassment behaviors and should be avoided. The supervisor should be careful in the choice of works and avoid terms such as *honey, cutie, good girl, good boy,* or other gender-based statements that could be somewhat belittling and disrespectful and potentially violate sexual harassment laws.

Another federal law that may impact the evaluation session is the Family Medical Leave Act of 1993. This law prohibits discrimination against employees who request time off for their own serious illness or that of a family member. This law may have implications in giving a performance rating to an employee, especially if the rating is less than satisfactory when there might have been an approved leave of absence by the employee. These types of performance issues are not always clear cut and demand careful thought by the supervisor. Other potential problems may be impacted by union agreement. For example, a contractual agreement may allow an employee to request a third party to be present during an evaluation session, especially when the evaluation is anticipated to be unfavorable to the employee.

SUMMARY

The professional development and evaluation of employees is one that requires a systematic and comprehensive knowledge in all aspects of human resource management. Understanding the myriad of state and federal laws and local school policies is critical in managing human resources. The proper mentoring and professional development of employees can help improve student achievement and contribute to high morale in the organization. Moreover, incorporating an effective performance evaluation system can help ensure that employees perform to the standards required by the organization and allow the school district to remain legally compliant.

There are numerous resources available to assist educators in this entire process and should be utilized to develop the best systems and processes that are relevant for an organization. Moreover, developing a collaborative approach with involvement by all stakeholders can help to ensure agreement and success to the recruiting and professional development programs.

CASE STUDY

You have been recently hired as the school principal for Johnson High School in the northwestern United States. The school has approximately 1,000 students and a teaching faculty who is fairly diverse in age, race, and gender. The academic performance of the students is average as compared to other school districts in the state. There has been significant involvement of one group of parents who do not represent the interests of the entire community. It seems they are more interested in pressuring the school district to hire more women teachers.

selection.

sel, best

The superintendent has also mentioned to you that the performance evaluation system is outdated and that some local area school districts have been using a new computerized appraisal system. He also mentioned that Johnson High School has never had a mentoring program since they have not needed to hire new employees for several years. Overall, the school board and superintendent have high hopes for you as a new principal.

The school board and superintendent have charged you, as the new principal, to submit five goals and a strategic action plan for the high school for the ensuing school year. Based upon the information in this case, please develop five goals and a strategic action plan.

EXERCISES AND DISCUSSION QUESTIONS

1. List the steps and characteristics for developing a comprehensive mentoring program at a school.
2. List and describe some of the relevant federal, state, and school laws and policies impacting the mentoring process.
3. List the characteristics of an effective teacher professional development program.
4. Outline the types of topics for a typical teacher professional development program.
5. List the five categories and examples for a professional development program.
6. Describe some major reasons for conducting performance evaluations.
7. Describe some of the typical problems in conducting a performance evaluation review session.
8. List and describe some of the pertinent federal and state Equal Employment Opportunity Commission laws when conducting a performance evaluation review session.
9. Outline the steps in conducting a comprehensive evaluation process.
10. List and describe five typical performance factors in a performance evaluation form.

REFERENCES

Bubb. S., & Earley, P. (2009). Leading staff development for school improvement. *School Leadership & Management, 29* (1), 23–37.

Preparation
Introd session
review all ratings
overall

reaction
signature
discuss agree goals
DOCUM / file

Cleveland, J., & Murphy, K. (1995). *Understanding performance appraisal.* Thousand Oaks, CA: Sage.

Desimone, L. (2011). A primer on effective professional development. *Phi Delta Kappan, 92* (6), 68–71.

Hanson, S. (2010). What mentors learn about teaching. *Educational Leadership, 67* (8), 76–80.

Milanowski, A. (2011). Strategic measures of teacher performance. *Phi Delta Kappan, 92* (7), 19–25.

Prather-Jones, B. (2011). Some people aren't cut out for it: The role of personality factors in the careers of teachers of students with EBD. *Remedial & Special Education, 32* (3), 179–91.

Simon, S. (2011). Characteristics of effective professional development for early career science teachers. *Research in Science & Technological Education, 29* (1), 5–23.

Sykes, G., & Dibner, K. (2009). Improve teaching quality with aggressive support. *Phi Delta Kappan, 90* (8), 588–91.

Civil Rights Act - 64
Age Discrum 67
ADA - 1990
Title VII - Sec 1604 - Sex Harass
FMLA 1993

4

Leading and Motivating Employees

OBJECTIVES

At the conclusion of this chapter, you will be able to:

1. Understand principles and theories of leadership (ELCC 1.2, 2.1, 3.1, 5.1, 5.2; ISLLC 1, 2, 3).
2. Understand principles and theories of motivation (ELCC 3.1, 5.1; ISLLC 1, 2, 3).
3. Describe principles of human resource leadership (ELCC 2.1, 5.1; ISLLC 1, 3).
4. Apply strategies for leading employees (ELCC 3.3; ISLLC 3).
5. Apply strategies for motivating employees (ELCC 3.1, 3.3, 6.1; ISLLC 3, 6).

PRINCIPLES OF LEADERSHIP

An effective human resources (HR) administrator needs to understand and practice effective leadership and motivation principles and strategies to maximize employee performance. There are many qualities of effective HR leaders, such as technical knowledge and fiscal, interpersonal, training, planning, and coaching skills needed to support the administrative team in achieving the goals of the organization (Smith, 2010). One important quality is the ability to establish a clear-cut vision for the HR function. A vision is a concrete plan that is different than a mission. A mission is a more general statement, and a vision is a more concrete one. Effective HR leaders have the ability to establish a clear-cut HR vision for the organization that supports both academic and operational performance. They also know how to measure the results of their vision and strategic goals (Tomal, 2007).

Another characteristic of an effective HR leader is that of *role modeling*. HR leaders often serve as the role model for employees and students, and these leaders need to understand and practice good behaviors that support the values of the organization. Good followers often make good leaders. The ability to effectively inspire employees and then to exhibit effective leadership characteristics is critical in modeling these characteristics for employees (Covey, 1991).

LEADING EMPLOYEES *Situational - Hersey/Blanchard*

One of the more popular leadership theories that has practical applicability to leading employees was developed by Paul Hersey and Kenneth Blanchard and titled *situational leadership theory*. This theory builds upon the situational leadership styles proposed by the authors, who develop a continuum of lead-

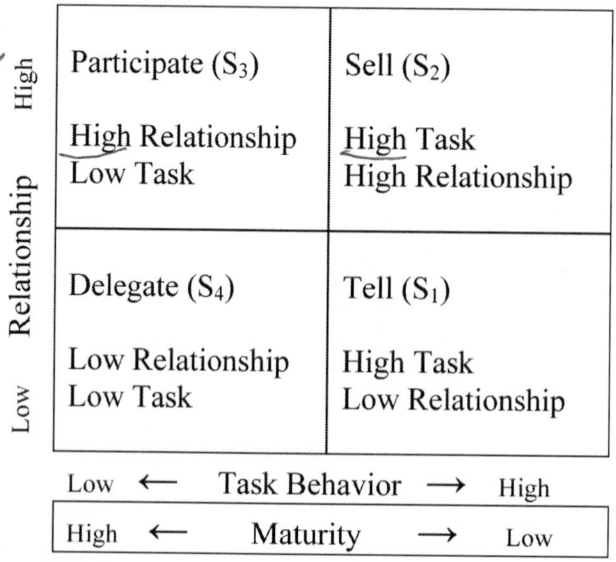

	Participate (S$_3$) High Relationship Low Task	Sell (S$_2$) High Task High Relationship
	Delegate (S$_4$) Low Relationship Low Task	Tell (S$_1$) High Task Low Relationship

High — Relationship — Low

Low ← Task Behavior → High

High ← Maturity → Low

EXHIBIT 4.1
Situational Leadership Model
Source: Hersey 1994.

ership behavior ranging from authoritarian to participatory (see exhibit 4.1). This theory can be valuable in helping leaders understand the best styles in leading employees. To understand this theory, there are several terms that need to be defined. *Task behavior* can be defined as one-way communication (directive behavior) from a supervisor to an employee. When a supervisor uses the task behavior, he or she is giving direct instructions to an employee. The task behavior is very directive, and there is basically no interchange or conversation. In this style, the employee is basically listening to the supervisor.

The term *relationship behavior* can be described as two-way communication between a supervisor and employee. The relationship behavior is very supportive, and this communication is a two-way discussion. This behavior also assumes that there is a high emphasis placed upon both talking and listening.

The term *maturity* can be described as the degree of an employee's positive attitude, experience, and overall emotional maturity in performing the job. The maturity levels are low, moderate, and high. If an employee has low maturity, he or she is considered to be immature. A high maturity level would describe an employee as being very mature in his or her attitude and behavior.

In the situational leadership model, there are four leadership styles. Style 1 (S_1) is called *telling*. In this style, the supervisor uses a high-task and a low-relationship behavior. This would be an example where the supervisor is giving one-way direction to an employee, and there is virtually no discussion. For instance, a principal could use this style when explaining the job requirements to a new administrative assistant on his or her first day of work. The second style (S_2) is called *selling*. This style uses high-task and high-relationship behaviors. In this style, the supervisor is engaging in directive conversation with an employee. This style considers that the maturity level of the employee is in between low and moderate. The next leadership style (S_3) is called *participating*. In this style, the supervisor uses high-relationship and low-task behaviors. This leadership style assumes that the maturity level of the employee is increasing and ranges between moderate and high. The last leadership style is called *delegating* (S_4). This style uses low-relationship and low-task behaviors. It also assumes the maturity level of the employee is high.

Let's examine an example of how a supervisor could use the situational leadership theory in leading an employee. If a supervisor has a new teacher assigned to a classroom, it can be assumed that the teacher will most likely have a low maturity given that he or she does not understand responsibilities and expectations. In this situation, the supervisor may begin using the style of telling. The telling style would assume that the teacher knows virtually nothing about the classroom assignment, and therefore, the supervisor would need to exhibit high-task and low-relationship behaviors. The supervisor would begin by explaining the assignment and expectations while the employee listens. There would be no need for two-way discussion given that the teacher initially would not need to have questions versus having the need to gain information. It should not be assumed that the telling style is an ineffective style but can be appropriate for a new teacher who has a very low maturity level.

As the teacher begins to mature and starts to understand the assignment and expectations, there becomes a need for both high-task and high-relationship behavior by the supervisor. In this situation, the supervisor would use the style of selling. This style assumes that there is two-way conversation with the teacher. For example, the teacher might begin asking questions and participate in conversation with the supervisor, even though the supervisor would still need to be somewhat directive in explaining the assignment and expectations of the job.

As the new teacher continues to mature and develops more of a moderate to high maturity level, the supervisor would then use the style of participating. The participating style assumes that there is a need for high-relationship and low-task behaviors. In this situation, the supervisor needs to continue to give respect to the teacher by engaging in a two-way conversation, and there is little need for the supervisor to be very directive.

As the teacher continues to mature and develops a high maturity level, the supervisor would then use the style of delegating. In this situation, there is a need for low-relationship and low-task behaviors. When the teacher has a high maturity level, the supervisor no longer needs to explain the assignment and expectations of the job because the teacher understands them and is considered very mature. The example of a new teacher and his or her maturity development provides an effective situation for a supervisor to utilize all four styles of situational leadership in an appropriate manner. While variations may occur in the teacher's maturity level, the supervisor should constantly be aware of assessing this maturity level and adapt his or her style appropriately.

 The situational leadership model takes in consideration three major aspects—the style of the leader, the employees being led, and the situation. For example, the situational leadership model does not indicate that there is only one right style; rather the model suggests that the supervisor should use the appropriate style given the situation and maturity level of the employees. For example, if a supervisor observes a staff member engaging in disruptive behavior, the supervisor most likely would resort to the leadership style of telling and would be very directive in asking the staff member to correct the behavior.

The telling style is often appropriate when a supervisor needs quick directive change in behavior. Another example where the telling style may be appropriate is in the case of an emergency. If there is a fire drill and directive instructions need to be given to all employees for their welfare, the supervisor would use the telling style. During an emergency situation, generally there is no need for two-way discussion, but rather the supervisor needs to act decisively in ensuring the safety of all employees and students by giving one-way instruction.

The selling leadership style is one that a supervisor may find very useful in needing to convince a staff member to improve his or her performance. When a staff member's performance needs to improve, using the telling style may create resentment, and the selling style may be best to establish a professional two-way discussion but at the same time it is firm and directive.

The participating leadership style can be effective when dealing with a staff member who has a moderate to high maturity level. For example, if a supervisor has a staff member who has a negative attitude, the two-way conversation may be the best leadership style. In this situation, the staff member is more apt to accept constructive feedback and improve.

The delegating leadership style can be very effective when dealing with a staff member who has a high maturity level. For example, if the staff member is working on a project and is fully capable of completing it, then the supervisor should back off and give the staff member the necessary authority and empowerment. The delegation style can be very effective in allowing high-maturity employees to make decisions without need for much interaction with the supervisor.

The main aspect of using situational leadership includes the notion that the supervisor needs to use the most effective style given the situation. For example, a supervisor may have a staff member who has a high maturity level and uses the delegation style. However, if the staff member begins to lose his or her maturity level and slips to a low level, then the supervisor may need to adjust his or her style accordingly. In this case, if the staff member now has a low maturity level, the supervisor may need to adapt to the telling style to correct the behavior.

A unique aspect of applying the situational leadership theory is its dynamic aspect. The supervisor may find him- or herself simultaneously using the telling, selling, participating, and delegating styles on a frequent basis. The supervisor may be using one-way directive (telling) behavior with an employee and then immediately switch to a participating style with another. The supervisor's ability to switch styles quickly is a key in successfully applying this theory. One danger for a supervisor in using this style is becoming dependent on using one style too frequently. A supervisor may become trapped in consistently using the telling style, and this style most likely will not be effective in dealing with all employees all the time. Likewise, if the supervisor only uses the delegating style, this could have devastating consequences. Employees who need direction may resort to poor performance without the proper leadership style.

One of the landmark theories in developing positive leadership was proposed by Douglas McGregor. He proposed a theory that centers upon the attitude of the leader. He suggested that leaders largely fall into one of two styles—*theory X* or *theory Y* (see exhibit 4.2). McGregor felt that leaders tend to make assumptions about their people. For example, he felt that a theory X leader assumes that people are lazy, irresponsible, and need to be coerced, controlled, and directed in order for them to perform work. He felt that theory X leaders view their workers as people who inherently dislike work and have little ambition.

X Leader	Y Leader
Dislikes work	Work is natural
Avoids work	Is productive
Needs to be coerced	Seeks work
Needs to be controlled	Seeks responsibility
Needs to be directed	Seeks learning
Needs to be threatened	Desires advancement
Not self-motivated	Is self-motivated

EXHIBIT 4.2
Theory X and Theory Y
Source: Adapted from McGregor, 1960.

The theory Y leader exhibits the opposite traits and assumptions from the theory X leader. The theory Y leader believes that people are creative, self-directed, desire to work, are responsible, and that work is important to them. Essentially, McGregor felt that the theory X leader is negative and that the theory Y leader is positive toward people.

McGregor's theory has wide implications for leading employees. For example, if a principal assumes the theory X assumption, then the principal tends to be very directive and threatening to the faculty and staff. The principal often develops a sarcastic attitude. The faculty and staff in turn often behave and perform accordingly. In other words, if you don't expect much, you don't get much. If people are treated as if they are lazy and irresponsible, then they often perform to the leader's expectations. While some administrators may not vividly exhibit theory X behavior, people can often pick up on subtle cues from the leader. If an administrator has tendencies of being a theory X leader, those subtle signs can be observed by people through gestures. For example, the administrator may have less eye contact with people or exhibit a frown, or the inflection of the administrator's voice can be clues that he or she has negative assumptions about the staff. Moreover, the subtle use of an administrator's nonverbals can be revealing. For example, if the administrator tends to point his or her finger and talk in a condescending manner toward the staff, these cues become very obvious and reveal the administrator's true assumptions.

The theory Y administrator is one who exhibits a positive attitude toward faculty and staff. This administrator promotes a healthy atmosphere and motivates people to perform their best. The administrator's assumption is to expect the best of the people, and they in turn will often perform to their expectations.

The most important significance of McGregor's theory is that the assumptions that administrators, as leaders, have toward their faculty and staff can create a *self-fulfilling prophecy.* The notion of the self-fulfilling prophecy is that a belief in an event or expectation can actually cause it to happen. Therefore, if leaders don't expect much from their employees, they will in turn not get much. On the other hand, if leaders place high expectations on people, then they will often perform to their high expectations. The concept of self-fulfilling prophecy can be seen in many aspects of life. In the sports arena, the concept of the self-fulfilling prophecy is widely used. If a coach places high expectations on his or her players, the players will often perform to those expectations. For example, if a coach removes a player from the game at a

Selling Particip   self-fulfilling prophecy
Telling delegating

critical moment because he or she does not believe the player can succeed and replaces the player with another player, these expectations can have reinforcing consequences. The player who is removed often will continue to perform ~~MCD~~ less, while the player who the coach has <u>confidence</u> in often improves his or her performance. The essence is that <u>success has reinforcing consequences.</u> The notion that <u>success breeds success</u> is supportive of the self-fulfilling prophecy. Therefore, whether the leader is a coach leading a sports team or a *note* teacher leading a group of students, the same concepts apply (Smith, 2009).

THE LEADERSHIP GRID *Blake & Mouton*

A very popular and classic leadership model is the theory called *the leadership grid* by <u>Blake and Mouton (1969; see exhibit 4.3)</u>. The leadership grid describes <u>five different leadership styles.</u> The general notion of this grid implies that all leaders make assumptions regarding *concern for production* versus *concern for people*. Concern for production implies that leaders have a very high-task directive desire for obtaining productivity. These leaders place higher value on achieving productivity versus concern for people. The left-hand side of the grid describes a scale for concern for people. This scale indicates the degree of concern for people by the leader. A low concern for

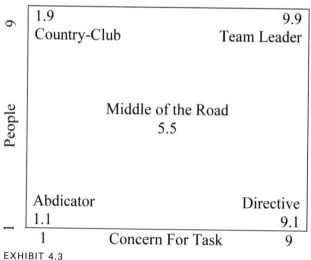

EXHIBIT 4.3
The Leadership Grid
Source: Blake & Mouton, 1985.

people would be the number 1, while a high concern for people would be the number 9. In this model, the relationship between concern for production and concern for people then can be plotted on the graph. The authors have actually devised instruments that measure a leader's concern for production and people and resultant dominant style.

The *abdicator* is one who exerts minimum effort and concern to either people or production. This type of leader can be described as an *impoverished leader*. He or she does not have regard for getting work accomplished, nor does he or she have much care for the feelings of people. This type of leader can sometimes be viewed as very apathetic and ineffective. For example, if a teacher is suffering from burnout and has negative feelings toward the school system and dislikes his or her students, he or she may adopt the style of the impoverished leader. This type of administrator may be very resentful toward both the staff and school and is simply waiting out his or her time in order to retire. This type of leader can be very damaging to a staff. Generally, this type of leader does not receive much respect, nor does he or she produce a healthy learning environment. The impoverished leader can be described as the 1.1 manager. This style indicates very low concern for people and production.

The *country-club leader* is a manager who is described as the 1.9. This type of leader has a very high concern for people but very low concern for production. This leader is more concerned about satisfying the needs of people than getting results. For example, this type of leader may give exceptionally high performance evaluation ratings to all employees in an effort to gain their favor. A typical example of this type of leader may be a new principal who desires to have the unconditional support of all of his or her teachers. While this type of leader may succeed in obtaining many friendships, he or she probably does not produce an enriching learning environment. As a consequence, the staff probably will not achieve at their highest level. Another example of the country-club leader could be a situation where an administrator has received many complaints from students and community and may feel that his or her job is in jeopardy, so he or she may resort to being overly friendly to the staff without regard to performance. While the country-club leader may not be as bad as the impoverished leader, nevertheless this style is probably very ineffective in achieving the best results from people.

The *middle-of-the-road leader* can be described as the 5.5 manager. This type of leader tends to have a balance between wanting to satisfy the needs of people and getting results. This type of leader can sometimes be viewed as straddling the fence because the leader has only moderate concern for people and production. An example of this leader could be an administrator who simply views his or her job as only a job and places only moderate effort in the concern for people or production.

The *directive leader,* or *authority-compliance leader,* is one who is most interested in getting results and has little regard to satisfy the needs of people. For example, this type of leader would be an administrator who is only concerned with getting high test scores at the expense of jeopardizing teacher relationships. They tend to be very directive and not very friendly toward teachers. This leader can be described as the 9.1 manager. While this type of leader is striving to obtain high test scores, the result may be less given his or her authoritarian style.

The *team leader* can be described as the 9.9 manager. This type of leader has a very high concern for people as well as production. The authors believe that this is the ideal style and that all leaders should strive to be the team manager. This style is described as work being accomplished through committed people and that everyone has trust and respect for each other. The authors emphasize that all leaders should strive to obtain the team leader style and that this can be a growing process as the leader matures and becomes more experienced.

One leadership model designed specifically for school leaders is called the *leadership capability model* (see exhibit 4.4). This leadership model illustrates four types of leaders depending upon the degree of the leader's competence and confidence (Tomal, 2007). In order to understand the model, three terms need to be defined. *Competence* refers to the leader's ability to effectively lead and motivate people. High competence indicates the leader's ability to understand both intrinsic and extrinsic motivators and how to effectively use these motivators in motivating people. Competence refers to the leader's effectiveness in understanding and applying the effective qualities of leadership and motivation.

The second term, *confidence,* indicates a leader's feelings of adequacy and self-reliance in leading and motivating people. A leader with high confidence suggests having strong spirit, tenacity, courage, and resolution with his or her ability as a leader. A leader who has low confidence would be apprehensive, having feelings of self-doubt and uncertainty in actually leading and motivating people.

The third term in understanding the model is *self-management.* Self-management refers to the leader's degree of experience, knowledge, and

resolute leaders

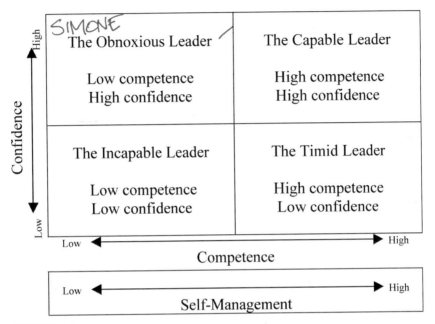

SIMONE

EXHIBIT 4.4
Leadership Capability Model

resourcefulness as a leader. Self-management indicates how "seasoned" the leader is in having a good self-concept and belief in his or her abilities as a leader. Self-management goes beyond only being competent or confident and suggests the quality of experience and fortitude in applying both confidence and competence in leadership.

In applying the leadership capability model to leading and motivating school employees, if a leader has low self-management and low competence and confidence, then this leader can be referred to as an *incapable leader*. The incapable leader would have the qualities of not being confident or competent in his or her ability to lead and motivate people. This leader would not have an understanding of leadership and motivational factors and would be ineffective in leading people.

A leader who has low self-management but also low competence and a high confidence could be referred to as the *obnoxious leader*. This leader, while having high confidence in leading and motivating people, does not have the competence and therefore may demotivate people. This typical leader is one who is undoubtedly assertive in attempting to lead and motivate people but is ineffective given the lack of knowledge and skills (i.e., competence).

The third type of leader is called the *timid leader*. This is a leader who may have high competence but lacks confidence in effectively leading and motivating people. While this leader may have high self-management in terms of understanding effective strategies for leading and motivating people, the leader is ineffective given his or her lack of confidence.

The fourth type of leader is the *capable leader*. This leader incorporates a high self-management (understands leadership and motivation strategies) and has both high competence and high confidence. This is an effective leader who is able to understand both intrinsic and extrinsic motivators and how to effectively apply them in motivating people given his or her high degree of self-assurance. The effectiveness of applying this model rests with the understanding that the term *self-management* refers to a leader's understanding of strategies and techniques for leading and motivating people. Being a capable leader goes well beyond just the understanding of leadership and motivational strategies but also requires the need for high confidence in order to be an effective leader. For example, if an administrator has a group of employees who are very apathetic and consistently demonstrate poor performance, then the possibility of the leader having both low confidence and competence may exist. This administrator, in essence, may be the incapable leader, and he or she needs to develop high self-management abilities in understanding leadership and motivational strategies and the competence in applying these strategies as well as the self-assurance. On the other hand, an administrator who may be very motivated and self-assured to apply strategies but lacks the actual competence would still have low self-management because of his or her inability to understand the leadership motivation strategies.

On the other hand, the administrator who can be described as the timid leader would be one who has a group of employees who may also have performance problems and high motivation. This timid leader may be very effective in writing the rules for performance standards but may have difficulty in actually applying the strategies given his or her low confidence. The capable leader most likely would have a group of employees who are motivated and have good performance due to his or her ability to communicate rules and procedures of good performance as well as the skills to apply these strategies in the work setting (Tomal, 2007).

MOTIVATING EMPLOYEES

"You can lead a horse to water, but you can't make him drink" is a familiar statement many leaders can relate to. *Motivation* is a difficult term to define. Essentially it is the willingness of a person to partake in an endeavor in order to satisfy a person's need (Poornima, 2009). Human beings have an innate desire to satisfy basic physiological and psychological needs. The ability to influence employees to be motivated to have a desire to achieve a goal is an overall objective of educational leaders (Nohia, Groysberg, & Lee, 2010). While there are many different educational theories regarding motivation, most of them have a common underlying theme regarding the human needs of people. Developing and understanding human needs can be very valuable in motivating employees (Brown, 2009).

Abraham Maslow (1943) articulated one of the first theories on human needs by classifying them into five different levels. The lower-order needs (first two levels) consist of basic physiological needs, including safety and security. The higher-order needs (upper three levels) consist of belonging and social needs, esteem and status needs, and self-actualization and fulfillment (see exhibit 4.5).

Need Level	Leader Motivation Strategies
Self-Actualization	Encourage work for work's sake
	Emphasize love of the job
	Encourage personal learning interests
	Encourage creativity and innovation
Esteem and Status	Give positive reinforcement
	Provide public praise and rewards
	Give frequent coaching
	Encourage responsibility
Social and Belonging	Promote collaboration
	Emphasize teamwork
	Promote interpersonal relations
	Encourage social activities
Safety and Security	Ensure safe work conditions
	Provide security
	Ensure consistent and fair treatment
	Provide safety cameras
Physiological	Provide basic benefits
	Emphasize proper sleep at home
	Allow breaks
	Ensure proper lighting and temperatures

EXHIBIT 4.5
Strategies for Motivating Employees Based on Human Needs

Maslow's hierarchy can be applied to motivating employees. People may seek different amounts of a certain need than others. Some individuals simply have a higher need for security than other people. For example, many people feel very insecure when living paycheck to paycheck. Some people are greatly affected by not having a savings account, while others feel that as long as they're not in debt everything is fine (i.e., they feel secure). Likewise, employees may have different need levels. Some employees simply may need more attention than others. Therefore, employees' desire to fill their human needs in the workplace involve a multiplicity of factors, such as peer group identification, sense of duty, collaboration, desire for a promotion, attitude toward the school board, and a need for attention and recognition. However, one thing is common: if these needs are not met, the employee's motivation will be affected. Understanding how to meet student human needs can help people to be more motivated and in turn effective.

The *two-factor motivation theory* proposed by Fredrick Herzberg (1966) is one of the more prominent theories of human motivation. While Herzberg primarily worked with industrial companies, his theories can also be applied to the education setting (see exhibit 4.6). Herzberg's model is similar to Maslow's hierarchy and provides a basis for understanding human motivation. Herzberg concluded that people experience good or bad feelings based upon different types of feelings based upon different types of conditions at work. He theorized that different factors will influence motivation based upon workers' views toward these motivation factors (Tomal, 2007).

Low motivation	Neutral	High Motivation
-1	0	+1

Extrinsic

Maintenance Factors
- Provide extrinsic rewards
- Ensure proper conditions
- Give raises
- Provide tangible tokens
- Ensure good policies
- Provide fair treatment

Intrinsic

Motivational Factors
- Emphasize love of the job
- Provide positive reinforcement
- Give verbal praise
- Provide advancement
- Give professional development
- Show appreciation for good work

EXHIBIT 4.6
Strategies Based on Herzberg's Two-Factor Motivation Theory

There are two predominant groups that Herzberg categorized—*maintenance factors* and *motivational factors*. Maintenance factors consist of relationships with supervisors, peer relations, quality of supervision, administrative company policies, work conditions, and reward structures. The maintenance factors are also called *extrinsic factors*. Extrinsic factors can be viewed as external types of rewards that can reinforce performance but are not found within learning itself. For example, an employee may be motivated to accomplish a job task because of the desire for an extrinsic reward, such as a bonus. This extrinsic factor, in essence, is the motivator that is stimulating the person to accomplish the task.

Motivational factors consist of work itself, the possibility of growth and advancement, responsibility, status within the organization, recognition, and achievement. Motivational factors can be considered as intrinsic factors. Intrinsic factors are significantly different in that the rewards are not tangible. *Intrinsic factors*, or intangible rewards, are given as a result of the work itself. For example, an administrator who has a love of education will be motivated in his or her job because of this intrinsic satisfaction. For example, in the business world, there are often people who are financially successful and could retire, but they would rather continue working because they obtain fulfillment in life. Likewise, teachers who obtain satisfaction from work will be motivated to continue their growth, development, and teaching career.

The two-factor theory of motivation can be applied to employees in a school. If employees' maintenance factors, such as school discipline policies, the administration of the policies, safety and security, and school conditions, are not met at a minimum level, employees can become dissatisfied and demotivated. The lack of clear-cut school policies and inconsistent administration of the policies can result in people being demotivated. Likewise, if an employee feels that the principal is ineffective, the employee can also be demotivated.

Much like workers in a company, once maintenance factors have been met for employees within a school, in order to provide the opportunity for them to become more motivated, motivational factors must be provided. These intrinsic motivational factors might include potential for growth and learning, peer recognition, awards and work achievement, status within the school, and the rewards of future promotion opportunities. If motivational factors are not provided, employees may never become motivated to grow to higher academic levels.

$$\text{Valence} \times \text{Expectancy} \times \text{Instrumentality} = \text{Motivation}$$

EXHIBIT 4.7
The Expectancy Motivation Model

The *expectancy motivational theory* is another landmark theory proposed by Victor Vroom (1964) that can be applied to the educational setting (see exhibit 4.7). Vroom theorized that human motivation is based upon the product of three factors: desire for reward (valence), belief that an effort will result in completion of a task (expectancy), and the knowledge that a reward will be obtained upon completion of the task (instrumentality.)

When applied to the school setting, *valence*, the first factor, can be viewed as a person's preference for receiving a good performance rating (i.e., reward). The person may strongly desire a good rating and will be highly motivated to perform. However, if the person lacks this desire and is indifferent, he or she will have a low valence, will not be motivated to achieve, and will consequently lack the motivation.

The second level, *expectancy*, can refer to a person's belief that his or her effort will result in the achievement of a desired task (i.e., successful completion of projects and work assignments). For example, if a person feels that higher-quality work will result in a better performance rating, then the person will spend more time on this goal. However, if the person feels there is not a direct relationship between quality work and a positive rating, he or she will be less motivated.

The third level, *instrumentality*, relates to a person's belief that a reward can be realistically obtained. For example, the person might believe that the principal is prejudiced against him or her, and no matter how well the person performs quality work, the person will never receive an excellent rating. In this case, the person's instrumentality will be low, and the result will be a low motivation.

Highly motivated employees need to have high levels of all three factors—valence, expectancy, and instrumentality. Vroom theorized that the strength of a person's drive to reach a goal is based upon the combination of these three factors, and a leader should strive to provide incentives for people. Likewise, the experiences employees obtain in the organization can directly contribute to their drive for each of these factors. Leaders can help provide these incentives by establishing work expectations and policies, fair and consistent evaluation, and proper reward structures (Webb, 2007).

The *equity motivation model* first proposed by Adams (1965) suggests that the motivation of people goes way beyond just satisfying their needs (see exhibit 4.8). This model suggests there is a direct relationship between how employees perform and how they value the rewards. Adams theorized that the issue of fairness applies to all types of rewards, such as social, economic, and psychological.

The premise of this model is that people will bring input into their work (e.g., personal commitment, time, desire, and energy) and expect to receive outcomes (e.g., money, praise, recognition, and benefits). People will analyze the degree of fairness of receiving their own outcomes as compared to the outcomes being received by others. The fairness, or equality, of these factors will be subjectively judged by the person. If the person believes that the outcomes (i.e., rewards) justify his or her degree of input as compared to others, then the person will be motivated. However, if the person feels that his or her outcomes are inadequate or unfair as compared to others, then the person will not be motivated (Goleman, 1995). For example, if an employee is contributing a high input but his or her performance rating is less than satisfactory as compared to his or her peers, an imbalance will result in the employee's perception. As a result, the employee may contribute less input to work.

Essentially the equity motivational theory explains that the motivation of a person is to avoid experiencing negative feelings that result from unjust treatment. These feelings result from the process of social comparison between people and coworkers. It is important to recognize that the reality of rewards may be different than the perception of the rewards. Employees often perceive rewards being higher to other people than themselves. The leader should recognize the equity motivation model in motivating people (Tomal, 2007).

Outcomes (compared with others)	Inputs (compared with others)
▪ Pay/Benefits	▪ Work Effort
▪ Special Rewards	▪ Learning Difficulty
▪ Psychological	▪ Performance

EXHIBIT 4.8
The Equity Motivation Model

SUMMARY

There are many leadership theories and models that administrators and human resource professionals can use to manage people. Some of the more popular ones include the Situational Leadership Theory, McGregor's X and Y Theory, the Self-Fulfilling Prophecy, Managerial Grid, and the Leadership Capability Model. These theories and models should be selected by administrators based upon the nature of the people being led, the situation, and the style of the leader.

There are also several motivation theories that can be used by administrators and human resource professionals to help inspire and motivate employees. Some of these include the Two-Factor Motivation Theory, Equity Model, and the Expectancy Motivation Theory. By using the various leadership and motivation theories and models, administrators and human resource professionals should have a good foundation for building a productive and high-performance human resource staff.

CASE STUDY

You are a new HR director at the Wilson Public High School, located in the southwestern United States. On the first day of your job, the superintendent scheduled a meeting with you to present several HR issues that currently exist at the school that need to be addressed. The superintendent has asked you to review each of these situations and to prepare a report to him as to how you plan to handle each of these issues. The issues are:

1. Employee 1—Henry has been a high school teacher with the district for over thirty years. He has been frequently sick lately, and his absenteeism is becoming a real problem. He has been a good teacher over the years, but lately he seems listless, quiet, and withdrawn.
2. Employee 2—Max is a second-year employee and holds the position of groundskeeper. He is single, and he likes to party. In fact, he is often seen showing off his new sports car to others while bragging about his late-night activities. The superintendent has noticed that he often sticks to himself at work and does not perform a thorough job in maintaining the school grounds. He seems to do the minimum job and nothing more. In fact, he has often been seen by the superintendent sleeping during his breaks or coming in at the last minute.
3. Employee 3—Kathy is an intelligent teacher with six years of experience and a high achiever. She finished her master's degree within the first two

years of teaching. She is constantly complaining to her colleagues and gives the impression that she doesn't feel motivated or challenged on the job as before. She also gives the impression that she is impatient with students, bored, and frustrated with the job.

4. Employee 4—Mark is assistant superintendent but is deep in debt, which is no surprise to anyone since he recently purchased a very expensive home, bought a new car, purchased elaborate furnishings, and got married. Since then, his home value has plummeted, and he is "under water" with his mortgage. He has revealed to the superintendent that he has many college loans and other outstanding bills because of his lavish lifestyle. He has only been an assistant superintendent for about two years, having been promoted fairly rapidly as a young teacher. His wife does not work, and it has been revealed that she is three months pregnant. He already has a three-year-old child from a previous marriage. It also didn't help matters when the superintendent stated he had overheard Mark talking to a friend in the lounge about his potential gambling problem. As far as his performance, the superintendent feels that he is doing a good job, but lately he seems to be distracted and is having a hard time concentrating and being motivated.

5. Employee 5—Jill is an attractive young administrative assistant who works in the school district office. Unfortunately she has just filed a sexual harassment claim against John, who is the director of special services for the district. She claims in the complaint that John has sent several sexually based e-mails to her. She also has stated that they used to date, but the relationship has soured. She claims that John is persistent in trying to salvage the relationship. He frequently calls her at her home in the evening. To make matters worse, she has stated that apparently while she was in John's private office, he inappropriately embraced her and gave her a kiss, although there were no witnesses. Following the complaint, Jill has been irate and has been making inappropriate comments about John and speaking poorly about him to her colleagues and even parents.

EXERCISES AND DISCUSSION QUESTIONS

1. Explain the leadership capability model that can be used for leading and motivated employees.

2. Explain Maslow's hierarchy and how this theory can be used in motivating employees in the school.

3. Describe Herzberg's two-factor motivation theory, and list several extrinsic (maintenance) factors and intrinsic (motivational) factors.
4. Describe the equity model and how it can be used for motivating employees in a school.

REFERENCES

Adams, J. (1965). Inequity in social exchange. In L. Berkowitz (ed.), *Advances in experimental pyschology*. New York: Academic Press, 267–99.

Blake, R., & Mouton, J. (1969). *Building a dynamic corporation through grid organization*. Reading, MA: Addison-Wesley.

Blake, R. R., & Mouton, J. S. (1985). *The managerial grid III: The key to leadership excellence*. Houston: Gulf Publishing.

Brown, J. (2009). Motivating your staff during a down economy. *Material Handling Management, 64* (5), 44–45.

Covey, S. (1991). *Principle-centered leadership*. New York: Simon & Schuster.

Goleman, D. (1995). *Emotional intelligence*. New York: Bantam Books.

Hersey, P. (1994). *The situational leadership*. New York: Warner Books.

Herzberg, F. (1966). *Work and the nature of man*. Cleveland, OH: World Publishing.

Maslow, A. (1943). A theory of motivation. *Psychological Review, 50*, 370–96.

McGregor, D. (1960). *The human side of enterprise*. New York: McGraw-Hill.

Nohia, N., Groysberg, B., & Lee, L. (2010). Employee motivation. *Harvard Business Review, 86* (7/8), 78–84.

Poornima, S. (2009). Motivating through satisfaction: An ongoing effort of HR in organizations. *ICFAI Journal of Management Research, 8* (5), 26–37.

Tomal, D. (2007). *Challenging students to learn: How to use effective leadership and motivation tactics*. Lanham, MD: Scarecrow Press.

Smith, D. (2010). A leadership skills gap? *T+D, 64* (2), 16–17.

Smith, S. (2009). Motivating employees in tough times. *EHS Today, 2* (8), 43–44.

Vroom, V. (1964). *Work and motivation*. New York: Wiley.

Webb, K. (2007). Motivating peak performance: Leadership behaviors that stimulate employee motivation and performance. *Christian Higher Education, 6* (1), 53–71.

5

Building Collaboration and Disciplining Employees

OBJECTIVES

At the conclusion of this chapter, you will be able to:

1. Understand principles of collaboration and teamwork (ELCC 1.2, 2.1, 3.1, 5.1, 5.2; ISLLC 1, 2, 3).
2. Understand principles of managing conflict (ELCC 3.1, 5.1; ISLLC 1, 2, 3).
3. Apply strategies for building collaboration and teamwork (ELCC 2.1, 5.1; ISLLC 1, 3).
4. Apply strategies for managing conflict (ELCC 3.3; ISLLC 3).
5. Understand principles for disciplining and terminating employees (ELCC 3.1, 3.3, 6.1; ISLLC 3, 6).

BUILDING COLLABORATION AND TEAMWORK

Collaboration and teamwork are critical synergistic characteristics of most organizations. Human resources (HR) administrators can play an important role in helping an organization create a positive culture of working together to achieve the vision of the school (Hartley, 2007).

Tuckman (1965) identified several stages of team development. HR administrators can consider these stages of development in promoting positive teamwork within the organization. The four stages include *forming, storming, conforming*, and *performing*. The forming stage can be considered the honeymoon stage. Employees are generally guarded, exchange pleasantries, and are somewhat respectful and cordial to each other. In this first stage, employees are still assessing their environment and the personalities of their coworkers. Employees also experience a degree of uncertainty regarding their relationships with their fellow coworkers and often assess the degree to which they have positive relationships.

In the second stage, storming, conflicts often emerge, and coworkers may bid for power and rebel against their leader as well as their fellow coworkers in an effort to gain power and recognition. The employees are attempting to find their place within the team and a sense of unwritten social order. Employees who emerge as winners often develop informal power and leadership positions within the school.

The third stage is called conforming and is sometimes referred to as the *norming* stage. This stage includes employees who establish standards of conduct and set norms for behavior. During this stage, employees for the most part will accept these rules and standards, however may still lack open support for each other.

The last stage, called the performing stage, is when the group is a high-functioning and proficient team. This stage allows group members to feel very supportive of each other with a sense of loyalty, and conflicts are managed constructively. When the leader is able to help a team achieve the highest level of performing, team members feel free to grow and learn and gain new learning experiences. It is at this stage where the group functions most productively and efficiently. The feelings of employees during this stage are very positive toward each other. People generally have a sense of "we" and collaboration with each other. Much like a good sports team, the feelings toward each of the team members are very cooperative and supportive as they all pursue a common goal (e.g., learning and development).

The leader can help the team members achieve the performing stage by identifying clear rules of conduct and a common purpose and by building trust and honesty, commitment, effective communications, appropriate conflict management, and recognition and reward systems. The leader is in essence the person who lays down the tracks and sets the example for the employees to follow. The leader cannot force the employees to become a high-functioning team but can provide situations that allow the employees to achieve high-performance teamwork (Tomal, 2007).

A leader's ability to be proactive versus reactive is critical for all administrators. *Proactive* leadership suggests the leader's ability to anticipate the

ANTICIPATE/

needs of employees and to take initiative in getting results (Mach, Dolan, & Tzafrir, 2010). The *reactive* leader is one who is content with the status quo, does not have the foresight to anticipate employee needs, and creates a working environment that is not vibrant and resourceful. A proactive leader is often one who is also service oriented. This leader recognizes his or her role as a leader in providing for the needs of others (Webb, 2007).

The notion of servant leadership is a moral value that entails a disposition of giving and altruism. The assumption that the leader is serving the needs of others is a key feature of moral and ethical leadership (Sergiovanni, 1990). The concept of moral leadership encourages learning that is based on moral and societal redeeming goals.

MANAGING CONFLICT

One of the important aspects in managing employees is the HR administrator's ability to manage conflict. HR administrators often have employees coming into their offices with complaints and conflicts with other employees. The leader's ability to effectively manage conflict has a direct relationship with the motivation of employees (Grensing-Pophal, 2010). There are several sources of conflict in schools. Conflict can result from poor communication, roles, territorial issues, goal incongruence, stress, poor procedures and policies, and ineffective leadership.

The perception or actual favoritism given to employees by supervisors can be a demotivating factor. This perceived or real favoritism is a form of preferential treatment in the eyes of the employee and can lead to disciplinary or performance issues. Administrators often are unaware of the perceived favoritism they may be giving to employees. The perception of favoritism can be as subtle as a mere lack of prolonged eye contact or the inflection of the administrator's voice to certain staff members in a department meeting. For example, an administrator may be more enthusiastic and positive to some people, which can be perceived as favoritism in the eyes of others. Therefore, administrators need to be aware of their communication and nonverbal behaviors toward all people and ensure that it is done uniformly.

The personality differences among employees can also be a source of conflict. Employees' personalities can be different and can lead to different preferences in approaching team exercises and also can lead to arguments. For example, if employees are working on a project and one employee has a personality of a *doer*, he or she may be more aggressive in wanting to more quickly accomplish the project when working with an employee with the *thinker* personality style. The thinker employee may feel that this employee is being too pushy and short minded concerning the project. Likewise, the employee's personality style of the *feeler* when working with the doer can cause conflict. The feeler may perceive the doer employee's personality as being insensitive toward him or her. Understanding these personality styles and application to the workplace can help in preventing and managing conflict situations in the workplace (Brogan, 2011).

Educators are constantly involved in school change to adhere to requirements of state and federal regulations. In addition, demands are often imposed on educators by parents, community members, school board members, and students. These demands, along with the need to constantly change, can cause stress and conflict. Managing change and adapting to change is a critical factor to employees. Stability can be the enemy of survival. Change is inevitable, and those who fail to effectively manage change can experience negative consequences.

The school environment can also contribute to conflict. If there is a great deal of noise and stimuli, employees may not adapt well to this environment and conflict may result. The work conditions may be distracting to employees, and their ability to focus on work can be hampered. An employee also may be impacted if the temperature of the environment is compromised. For example, if the temperature is either too hot or too cold, employees may have a difficult time focusing on work and begin to displace negative feelings to others.

One of the contributors of conflict is that of miscommunication among people. Human beings are social creatures and communicate on a daily basis. Each of their interactions often involves a negotiating element that leaves room for miscommunication to take place. For example, if a supervisor makes a statement to an employee and it is misunderstood, the supervisor may have ill feelings toward the person, and conflict can arise. Likewise, miscommunication can take place among administrators. In addition, there are many forms of communication, such as written, verbal, and nonverbal, which impact an employee's understanding of rules, regulations, and policies. For example, if information is communicated to an employee regarding work policies and procedures, the misinterpretation of the information may have a negative effect upon the person's performance, and conflict can be generated. Likewise, one of the most significant factors impacting upon miscommunication is that of the "grapevine" communication network. There is an informal communication system called the grapevine in schools in which rumors start and contribute to misunderstandings and miscommunication.

Some strategies to help HR administrators resolve conflict include:

- Understand the root cause and context of the conflict.
- Help people understand that there is more than one viewpoint on a matter.
- Negotiate collaboratively with the parties by examining areas of agreement and disagreement.
- Focus on the conflict issues, and avoid attacking the person or becoming emotional.
- Be an active listener, and acknowledge the feelings of other.

DISCIPLINING AND TERMINATING EMPLOYEES

Administering discipline to an employee is one of the most uncomfortable and difficult aspects of the supervisor's job. Rarely do supervisors administer discipline without the HR department being involved. All schools have rules and regulations that must be followed and respected by all employees. While *discipline* used to be a term that had a negative connotation, many HR directors strive to implement a corrective action program rather than a punitive one. Most discipline programs are called *progressive discipline* plans and follow a sequence of actions for disciplinary offenses. Some factors need to be taken into consideration before administering disciplinary action, such as the severity of the offense and if there are mitigating circumstances. HR directors must demonstrate due diligence in handling disciplinary offenses. Moreover, many school districts have a union contract that contains specified procedures on handling disciplinary offenses.

There is a broad range of misconduct that is prohibited by employees that is special to the school organization. Not only do policies and procedures apply to employees during the normal workday, but given the profession of a teacher, the actions of teachers outside the school hours may apply as well. Also, most school districts take into consideration mitigating or extenuating circumstances for disciplinary offenses. These may include the length of employment, past disciplinary record, performance, health issues, attitude of the employee, potential associated disabilities that might have contributed to the offense, and external extenuating factors that might have impacted or contributed to the offense.

POLICY
EMP- UNIF CODE

Also, many school districts working with the union may classify the offense into groups depending upon the seriousness of the conduct. These groups range from minor disciplinary acts to very serious, repeated, or flagrant acts of misconduct. "Examples of Disciplinary Offenses" lists some of the typical employee disciplinary offenses.

Examples of Disciplinary Offenses

1. Wasting time
2. Insubordination, refusal to do a job assignment
3. Improper dress
4. Unsatisfactory work performance
5. Lying to a parent or administrator
6. Possession of a gun on the school premises
7. Using obscene gestures or language
8. Reading a novel while instructing students
9. Falsifying a timecard
10. Leaving school without permission
11. Felony conviction while off the job
12. Theft of school property
13. Abusing school equipment
14. Unauthorized soliciting during school hours
15. Oversocializing on the cell phone
16. Bringing alcohol on school property
17. Sleeping on the job
18. Intimidating another coworker
19. Possession of or showing sexual magazines
20. Possession of drugs
21. Forgery
22. Harassment of an employee
23. Smoking on school premises
24. Extortion or assault
25. Vandalism or criminal damage
26. Battery
27. Gambling during school hours

When a disciplinary offense has occurred, it is important that the HR director conduct a thorough investigation. Investigations should utilize scru-

Step	Description
Situational analysis—Understand the disciplinary offense	Obtain background information, get all the facts, isolate behaviors, and pinpoint times and places.
Case analysis—Who, what, where, when, and why	Document the facts, such as working conditions, equipment that might have been used, job site, hour of the day, witnesses, people involved, motives, emotions, symptoms, and underlying causes that might have contributed to the disciplinary offense.
Summarize the facts	Summarize the pertinent information related to the disciplinary incident. Note all special and unusual conditions that might have warranted behavior or extenuating circumstances.
Talk to the discipline offender and others	Conduct a disciplinary fact-finding hearing with the offender and all people involved to document all information.
Render a conclusion	Summarize your conclusion as to the offense mitigating circumstances, offender's past performance, and legal and union considerations, and decide on the action to be taken.
Administer the judgment	Hold a meeting with the offender, and render the corrective action being administered after obtaining approval from administration or school board.
Documentation	Document all information and follow up in accordance with district policy.

EXHIBIT 5.1
Steps in Rendering Disciplinary Action

key

tiny, analysis, and insight prior to rendering a decision. Some of the reasons why investigations fail include jumping to conclusions, hearing only one side of the problem, failing to be objective, being persuaded by one or two dominant people, failing to follow school policy or union contract, or writing decisions based upon assumptions versus the facts. Exhibit 5.1 shows the steps in conducting a thorough disciplinary investigation.

When taking disciplinary action against an employee, there are several considerations that can be taken into account in rendering a decision:

- Punishment or retribution—This generally entails the need to punish the employee for committing a disciplinary offense.

- Deterrents—This factor may be considered to prevent others from engaging in similar conduct.
- Correction or reform—This factor may be considered when necessary to change the attitude or behavior of an employee.
- Legal considerations—This factor may need to be considered to uphold laws that require disciplinary action be taken against an employee for certain offenses.

corrective

Most school districts employ a *progressive discipline system*. The purpose of progressive discipline is to take a corrective approach in helping the employee understand the performance issue and provide opportunities for improvement. The primary goal is to improve the employee's performance. It is meant to be a fair system that employs substantial documentation and discussion with the employee. In most cases when disciplinary action is rendered, a performance improvement plan should be designed collaboratively with the employee so that the behavior can be corrected. Depending upon the gravity of the offense, the typical stages of progressive discipline in the workplace include:

FAIR

1. Casual counseling,
2. Verbal warning,
3. Written warning,   *reprimand*
4. Suspension, and
5. Termination.

The first stage of progressive discipline is generally not considered the first formal step in the process. *Casual counseling* implies the supervisor talking to the employee and providing minor coaching in order to correct a very minor offense. This step can be considered more of a warning to the employee and does not necessarily need to be documented in the HR file. An example could be where a teacher walks into the classroom as the bell is ringing, having grammatical errors in a lesson plan, using a cell phone during inappropriate times, or displaying a poor attitude toward students. Supervisors need to use discretion when considering whether to administer casual coaching or a verbal warning to an employee for an offense.

The *verbal warning* is technically the first formal stage of the progressive disciplinary program. The verbal warning is followed by a written documentation that is placed in the employee's file. Generally, if the offense or similar offense does not occur within a specified period of time (e.g., one year) based on district policy or union agreements, the employee then reverts back to formal standing. However, if the same or similar offense occurs by the employee, then generally, depending on circumstances, a *written warning* would be administered to the employee and documented in the file. This process would continue until the employee is *terminated* or reverts back to normal standing, depending upon the district policy or union agreement.

There are situations depending upon the gravity of a serious offense whereby an employee may be immediately discharged and all of the preceding stages would be skipped. Examples of terminating an employee based on cause might include indecent exposure, extortion, assault and battery, theft of school property, robbery, arson, engaging in a sexual activity, use of severe intimidation, possession of drugs, falsifying school records, forgery, gross civil disobedience, insubordination, rape, cheating, or falsifying student test scores.

Prior to terminating an employee, an administrator should always conduct a thorough investigation, consult the HR director, and obtain school board and union approval. Often when an alleged offense has occurred, the employee is sent home with or without pay pending a decision by the school board and administration. Besides committing an offense, other causes that may result in the termination of an employee may include physical or mental conditions that render the employee unfit to work. There are published federal and state laws on schools' HR that administrators need to follow.

When a tenured teacher is terminated, there are generally specified conditions that must occur during the process. Some of these include formal notification to the employee of the alleged charge and potential action, specified time periods known as statutes, and specific termination proceedings that often include a hearing for the charge, school board agreement, opportunity for legal counsel and witnesses, and possible open public forum and recorded hearing.

When a teacher is terminated due to cause, the teacher's license may be revoked by the state department of education. Generally the revocation of a teacher's license is based upon serious conduct, such as immorality, negligence of duty, insubordination, incompetence, mental illness, or egregious behavior. One concept that can negatively affect the outcome of a termination decision is called *group think*. Group think, as theorized by Irving Janis (1972) in the book *Victims of Group Think*, is when group members can try to minimize conflict and reach consensus without adequately analyzing and providing critical analysis in an effort to strive for unanimity. This term, *group think*, was first coined by William Whyte in 1952 in a *Fortune* magazine article. The symptoms of group think may include illusions of invulnerability, rationalization, stereotyping, self-censorship, direct pressure, and illusions of unanimity among the group members. Essentially, group think is a faulty decision-making process that can occur any time a group of members needs to make a decision, especially when under stress, budgetary constraints, isolation, or time constraints.

Group think may be exasperated when there is a more directive leader and compliant members. Therefore, when working as a team to make disciplinary or termination decisions for an employee, the group leader should encourage critical evaluators, consider inviting outside experts into the meeting, thoroughly examine alternatives, and encourage independent thoughts and free opinions prior to rendering a group decision (Janis, 1972).

With all disciplinary matters, laws and policies need to be followed prior to rendering disciplinary action or terminating an employee. For example, while drunkenness may be a cause for termination, it is sometimes difficult to prove the frequency of drinking and whether the drunkenness is related to an illness of alcoholism. Health practitioners may consider alcoholism a disease, and the employee may be protected by the Americans with Disabilities Act. Another example might relate to a teacher who is found sleeping on the job. There are a number of common sleep disorders, such as insomnia, hypopnea syndrome, narcolepsy, cataplexy, and dyssomnias. Many of these disorders cause chronic sleeping dysfunction, varying degrees of insomnia, anxiety, and underlying health conditions. Therefore, a supervisor should not jump to conclusions in charging the employee for a violation when an underlying medical condition may exist that would protect him under the Americans with Disabilities Act and other laws.

SUMMARY

All school leaders should be responsible for building collaboration and disciplining employees. HR directors and supervisors need to understand the principles, strategies, and current laws and policies in managing people. Moreover, the ability to effectively manage and resolve conflicts and build a collaborative and positive work environment is crucial for effectively operating the school. Also, the job of disciplining and terminating employees is not one to be taken lightly. There are many legal considerations that must be examined prior to taking action against employees. However, patience, due diligence, and knowledge of laws and district policies and procedures can help ensure that HR directors and school administrators can effectively manage the school.

CASE STUDY *Union*

You are a new HR director at Washington Public Elementary School, located in Oregon. On the first day of your job, the principal scheduled a meeting with you to present four major HR issues that currently exist at the school that need to be addressed. She has asked you to review each of these situations and prepare a report to her as to how you plan to address these issues. The issues are:

— role of Principal

1. There is significant conflict among the teachers. Many teachers avoid each other, and there has been open hostility in some of the departments.
2. There is not a defined disciplinary procedure or policy, and the union has been raising this issue for months. The union is threatening a formal charge if not addressed.
3. A maintenance worker was discharged for poor performance a week ago. Several employees feel this was a wrongful discharge and have been protesting. The union is also backing the discharged employee and plans to confront the issue.
4. There are a few teachers who are not performing well. There have been several complaints by other teachers, parents, and students.

observ feedback post conf—

EXERCISES AND DISCUSSION QUESTIONS

1. Explain Tuckman's four stages for team development, and list examples for each stage.
2. List the typical stages in the progressive disciplinary model.
3. List examples of disciplinary offenses that might warrant termination.

4. Describe the group think theory and how this theory could produce negative consequences in group decision making when terminating an employee.

5. Explain four reasons for disciplining employees.

REFERENCES

Brogan, J. (2011). Conflicting management paradigms. *Industrial Management, 53* (4), 26–30.

Grensing-Pophal, L. (2010). A good team. *Credit Union Management, 33* (5), 34–37.

Hartley, S. (2007). Motivating workers. *Businessdate, 15* (1), 1–3.

Janis, I. (1972). *Victims of group think.* Boston: Houghton Mifflin.

Mach, M., Dolan, S., & Tzafrir, S. (2010). The differential effect of team members' trust on team performance: The mediation role of team cohesion. *Journal of Occupational & Organizational Psychology, 83* (3), 771–94.

Sergiovanni, T. (1990). *Value-added leadership.* San Diego: Harcourt Brace.

Tomal, D. (2007). *Challenging students to learn: How to use effective leadership and motivation tactics.* Lanham, MD: Scarecrow Press.

Tuckman, B. (1965). Developmental sequence in small groups. *Psychological Bulletin, 63.*

Webb, K. (2007). Motivating peak performance: Leadership behaviors that stimulate employee motivation and performance. *Christian Higher Education, 6* (1), 53–71.

6

Benefits and Compensation

OBJECTIVES

At the conclusion of the chapter, you will be able to:

1. List and describe the different types of exempt and nonexempt salary schedules (ELCC 3.1, 3.2, 3.3; ISLLC 3).
2. Describe the Health Insurance Portability and Accountability Act of 1996 (ELCC 3.1; ISLLC 3).
3. Describe different types of compensation for school human resources (ELCC 3.3; ISLLC 3).
4. List and describe the various benefits common to school human resources (ELCC 3.1, 3.2, 3.3; ISLLC 3).
5. Describe a typical employee union and school board collective bargaining process (ELCC 6.3; ISLLC 3).
6. List and describe various tactics and counter-tactics used in the negotiation process between the school board and union (ELCC 2.2, 6.1; ISLLC 3, 6).
7. List and describe the responsibilities of a school negotiation team (ELCC 5.1; ISLLC 3).
8. List and describe the major components of the collective bargaining agreement (ELCC 3.3, 5.1, 6.1; ISLLC 3, 6).

ESTABLISHING A COMPENSATION PLAN

The operation of a school is a big business. Employees need to be compensated for the work they do, and compensation and benefits are the greatest proportion of a school district's budget (Flannery, 2010). It is estimated that over 80 percent of a school board budget is allocated to compensation alone (United States Bureau of Statistics, 2012). With this in mind, creating a fair compensation plan can have a great impact upon the fiscal health of the organization, recruiting, retention, and motivation of all employees. Unlike a private corporation, a school district cannot easily generate increased revenue or cut expenses. Many of the costs of running a school are fixed, and the amount of revenue is dependent upon state legislators, the federal government, and local taxpayers. The impact of different types of compensation on teacher performance and student learning has been examined for years with much controversy.

The business of public teaching is different from operating a private business. Educators work with the students they receive and are required to educate them and are not delivering services or producing products for a profit. Therefore the uniqueness of the role of the school needs to be considered when designing the best compensation plan for a school district.

There are many types of compensation plans used in organizations today (Sclafani, 2010). Many school systems use different plans for *classified nonexempt* or *nonclassified exempt* staff. Classified nonexempt staff includes positions such as food services, technology support staff, maintenance and custodians, transportation people, warehouse and distribution, secretaries, purchasing agents, accountants, and school instruction support. These employees often are paid an hourly rate and through use of a single-rate pay schedule. Classified nonexempt employees often are paid by this flat-rate approach and differ from exempt positions in that they are allowed by most laws to receive pay for overtime work. Exhibit 6.1 illustrates a typical salary schedule whereby each position is listed with several advancing step positions. The wage amount is often determined by completing a job evaluation. The job evaluation takes into consideration many different aspects, such as knowledge and experience, verbal and written skills, job complexity, mental and physical demands, supervisory responsibility, the work environment, and so on.

Many school districts use a point-factor system to evaluate each job position based upon predetermined factors in order to build a classification struc-

Years	BA	BA+15	MA	MA+15	MA+30	MA+45
1	$43,000	$45,900	$48,906	$49,560	$51,225	$52,455
2	$46,244	$47,465	$50,583	$51,812	$53,786	$55,018
3	$47,919	$49,250	$53,686	$54,574	$56,349	$57,680
4	$50,137	$51,468	$56,349	$57,680	$59,011	$60,342
5	$52,375	$53,686	$59,111	$60,342	$62,117	$63,004
6	$54,574	$55,905	$61,673	$63,004	$64,779	$66,110
7		$58,123	$64,335	$65,666	$67,541	$68,772
8			$66,997	$68,328	$70,103	$71,434
9			$69,659	$70,990	$72,765	$74,096
10			$72,321	$73,653	$75,427	$76,578
11			$74,987	$76,315	$78,089	$79,421
12			$77,646	$78,977	$80,752	$82,083
13			$80,308	$81,639	$83,514	$84,745
14			$82,970	$84,301	$86,076	$87,851
15			$86,276	$87,407	$89,182	$90,956

EXHIBIT 6.1
Example of a Teacher Salary Schedule

ture. In addition, many school district administrators compare their salary schedule with other school districts by conducting a salary survey. The use of outside employment consulting firms is sometimes used to obtain salary information. The criteria often used to make comparisons include school districts with similar community economic status, household income, number of students, and whether the school is an urban or rural institution.

One of the purposes of conducting a market survey is to create benchmark positions so that the school may decide what percentile of the range for each of these benchmarks they would like to achieve. Often a statistical regression analysis is conducted to create the salary progressions. For example, some schools may desire to be at the 80th percentile of the benchmark. When conducting the market salary survey, comparison of the total compensation package is typically done. Exhibit 6.2 illustrates many of the benefits of a complete employee compensation program.

Other aspects of a market salary survey include pay for holidays, floating holidays, bereavement pay, whether the school district has automatic across-the-board salary increases, merit and bonus plans, wellness programs, employee appreciation programs, incentives for bilingual skills, and so on.

Advanced degree stipend	Medical care	Sabbatical leave
Tuition Reimbursement	Dental care	Personal leave
Shift differential pay	Prescription drugs	Sick leave incentive plan
Cost of living adjustment	Vision care	Back pay of sick days
Severance Pay	Group life insurance	Jury duty
Tax-sheltered annuity plan	Long term disability insurance	On-call pay
Equipment allowances	Professional liability insurance	Stand-by time pay
Uniform allowances		Commission

EXHIBIT 6.2
Examples of Employee Benefits

SALARY STRUCTURES

When establishing the pay for a job position using the job factor system, points are assigned for each of the factors based upon the degree of complexity. For example, exhibit 6.3 illustrates a typical job evaluation form. In this form, an evaluation is completed by the market evaluator through such actions as interviews with existing employees, analysis of comparable job descriptions, review of existing performance appraisal systems, examination of current compensation structures, and so on. The purpose of this comprehensive study is to develop a complete and fair compensation program. Based on this information, a modification of the existing compensation system is generally completed.

For example, exhibit 6.3 illustrates a typical classified nonexempt maintenance position for determining the associated physical and mental job activities and environmental conditions for the position. The evaluator would actually rate each of the job activities using a scale from 1 to 7. When completed, the total points for each job position are tabulated. Exhibit 6.4 shows an example of a job evaluation tabulation of points for a job factor system. In this example, there are seven job factors that are being evaluated. They consist of knowledge, verbal complexity, written complexity, technology, supervisory responsibility, physical demands, and work conditions. There are four positions that are being evaluated, which are finance director, assistant

Rate this job by assigning a point value (1-7) for the job activities and work conditions.

Frequency Scale (1-7)

1 = Never
2 = One-to-Three hours per week.
3 = Four to 10 hours per week.
4 = Frequent: 10 to 20 hours per week.
5 = Very Frequent: 20 to 30 hours per week.
6 = Continuous: 30 to 40 hours per week.
7 = Constant: 100% of the week.

Physical Work	Frequency
Standing	
Sitting	
Walking	
Running	
Climbing and Lifting	
Stairs or Ladders	
Lifting 0 – 10 lbs.	
Lifting 11 – 20 lbs.	
Lifting 21 lbs. or more	
Bending, Squatting	
Repetitive Movement	

Environmental Conditions	Frequency
Using Hazardous Equipment	
Using Equipment	
West Surroundings	
Loud Noises	
High Temperatures	
Poor Ventilation	
Dust or Fumes	
Working Outside	

EXHIBIT 6.3

Evaluating a Job Position Using a Frequency Scale for Job Activities and Work Environment

Job Factor	Finance Director	Assistant Finance Director	Accountant	Payroll Clerk
Knowledge	1,500	1,200	800	500
Verbal Complexity	400	400	280	265
Written Complexity	300	250	155	130
Technology	300	300	250	150
Supervisory Responsibility	375	150	25	0
Physical Demands	30	30	30	30
Work Conditions	10	10	10	10
Total Points	2,915	2,340	1,550	1,085

EXHIBIT 6.4

Job Evaluation Tabulation of Points for a Job Factor System

finance director, accountant, and payroll clerk. The evaluator assesses each of these job factors per job position and assigns a point value for each of them. The total points are then calculated at the bottom of the form for each of the job positions. The idea behind using a job factor point system is to attempt to establish a fair and just pay schedule based upon the complexity and work conditions of a job.

Many jobs are classified according to a pay grade dependent upon the complexity of each job position. Some administrators assign a pay grade per job title and then aspire to pay each position at the benchmark percentile amount based upon average market data. A midpoint position with pay amounts that are 20 percent below and above the midpoint can also be established. This concept implies that a job is only worth so much money. When employees are hired, they generally start at the low end and gradually progress to the maximum end of the midpoint range. To achieve higher pay than the midpoint, employees need to produce high-performance through superior-performance appraisal ratings.

Once an employee reaches the top 20 percent range, typically he or she may not obtain additional merit increases but may be limited to cost-of-living adjustments. The theory of this system is that a job is only worth so much money. If an employee desires to achieve more money, then he or she needs to advance to a higher level through promotion. Exhibit 6.5 illustrates an example of establishing salaries compared to market salaries with 20 percent below and above benchmarks.

Grade	Minimum 20% Below	Midpoint	Maximum 20% Above
5	$37,384	$46,730	$56,076
6	$40,436	$50,545	$60,654
7	$43,737	$54,671	$65,605
8	$47,308	$59,135	$70,962
9	$51,170	$63,962	$76,754
10	$55,347	$69,184	$83,021
11	$59,866	$74,833	$89,800
12	$64,754	$80,942	$97,130
13	$70,041	$87,551	$105,061
14	$75,758	$94,698	$113,638
15	$80,000	$100,000	$120,000

EXHIBIT 6.5
A Competitive Job Grade for Midpoint and 20 Percent Below/Above Amounts

Teacher salary schedules tend to utilize the single-salary schedule, which is based upon the concept of a knowledge-based pay structure. The concept is that a teacher should be paid based upon their knowledge level for the job. There is an incentive then induced to increase one's knowledge level to increase one's pay. In this system, the teacher would achieve greater pay for each year of employment based upon the level of education. While this type of schedule is fairly common within public schools in the United States, it has been controversial. Many people feel that this system encourages further education but may have little to do with the actual performance of the teacher or impact on student learning. A teacher may advance in educational level but may not be able to transfer the knowledge to the student's performance. Likewise, a positive correlation may be difficult to establish for length of teaching experience and quality instruction. Just because a teacher has taught for thirty years does not necessarily make the teacher a better educator than one who has taught for five years. Simply stated, some people might feel that this system rewards teacher employment longevity versus teacher performance. These types of systems have prompted educators to examine alternative forms of compensation that may be fairer and have a more direct impact on achieving performance results.

TYPES OF COMPENSATION PLANS

There are many different types of compensation plans used in organizations today. Some of these consist of profit sharing, gain sharing, merit based, bonus based, non-cash recognition programs, deferred compensation, pay for performance, and so on. There is no one best compensation system, and school districts need to establish what works best for their exempt and nonexempt employees (Billinger, 2007). Also, people do not work for pay alone, and other rewards should be considered as part of the entire compensation package. For example, intrinsic rewards, such as having a career progression, job enrichment, the work itself, and full appreciation for the work being done, can have significant motivational impact for employees. On the other hand, in the absence of good working conditions, benefits and supervision can demotivate employees as well. All these factors should be taken into consideration. In other words, simply paying people more money may not guarantee higher performance or good results with student learning (Caillier, 2010).

A report completed by WorldatWork (2010) reveals some interesting statistics:

- There is a wide variety of pay practices and compensation systems, and nine out of ten companies subscribe to a compensation philosophy, with over 60 percent having a written policy and 29 percent having an unwritten policy.
- Forty-two percent of employees indicate that they do not understand their company compensation philosophy, and for the employees who understand the philosophy, they believe a written policy has a positive effect on employees' understanding.
- There is a higher attrition rate associated with companies who have unwritten compensation policies, suggesting that clearly establishing salary schedules and policies have benefits for employee retention.
- Nearly all organizations give a pay increase with a promotion and award merit increases for good performance (WorldatWork, 2010).

The objective of merit compensation plans is to coordinate an employee's performance with their compensation (Sawchuk, 2010). Many believe that providing merit pay based on performance provides an incentive to perform well and is a fairer compensation structure that may have a more direct impact on quality of work and student learning. However, determining merit pay requires subjectivity, and these plans are often criticized because of supervisory favoritism, disparities in amounts of money available, poor performance appraisal evaluations, and small differentiations between merit pay and performance. Unless there is a sufficient pool of merit pay to distribute, this plan may create employee dissatisfaction. For example, if an average performer receives a 2 percent merit pay and an exceptional performer receives a 3 percent pay raise, the difference may not be worth the additional work. Therefore, establishing a larger differentiation in merit pay among the levels of performance may be more motivating and fair to employees. Also, some compensation experts believe that the merit pay system in itself can produce aggressive competition among employees and undermine collaboration and teamwork. Employees soon realize that their merit pay is determined based upon their performance as compared to other employees. Also, employees may not be motivated by money alone and may not have a desire to work significantly harder to obtain more money. Some employees may be content with their current pay rate and level of job performance.

A gain-sharing compensation program is another option. The idea behind this program serves to reward employees who take responsibility and meet or exceed organizational goals. The program often works when clear organizational goals are established and employees then strive to meet or exceed these goals. Advantages of this type of program are that it helps organizations achieve sustained increases in results, employees have more accountability in achieving organizational goals, they share in the benefits, and there may be enhanced commitment for collaboration and teamwork and school district support. However, there can be many disadvantages to this type of program, such as not all employees are able to directly impact the accomplishment of goals, goals are not always easily measured, federal and state Fair Labor Standards Act guidelines may conflict with the plan, and the formulas for determining gain sharing may be complex. However, the combination of gain-sharing plans when constructed in a simplified manner can be beneficial for increasing motivation and productivity in achieving organizational goals of a school district.

Federal Laws	Description
Fair Labor Standards Act (FLSA), 1938	Provides provisions and guidelines for minimum pay, overtime, child labor, and fair compensation for equal work.
Equal Pay Act, 1963	Prohibits discrimination between employees on the basis of sex by paying wages to employees for equal work on jobs performed under similar working conditions.
Civil Rights Act, Title VII, 1964	Prohibits discrimination in compensation on the basis of race, color, religion, national origin, sex, and disability as amended.
Freedom of Information Act (FOIA), 1966, Amended 1974	Requires government agencies to provide access to certain compensation information of public school districts as requested by the public.
Age Discrimination in Employment Act, 1967	Prohibits discrimination in employment and compensation for people age forty and above.
Health Insurance Portability and Accountability Act (HIPAA), 1996	Guarantees certain health insurance coverage to employees and family with preexisting medical conditions.

EXHIBIT 6.6
Examples of Laws Impacting Compensation Programs

There are several federal and state laws that impact compensation programs (Sparks, 2010). Exhibit 6.6 lists some of the typical laws impacting compensation programs. Many federal and state laws protect employees from employment and compensation discrimination. Human resource (HR) administrators need to proceed with caution and due diligence in constructing fair and nondiscriminatory compensation programs that do not violate federal and state laws and union agreements.

Administering pay raises should be done fairly. Supervisor subjectivity in rating employees, especially for those who are protected class members, needs to be fair and nondiscriminatory. Also, the ability for the school board to pay given the fiscal condition of the school district can be a daunting task. Since most school district salaries account for over 80 percent of the school budget, any decrease in money can result in the need to terminate employees.

In many states an increase in revenue can only be achieved through successful tax levies, which are dependent upon local taxpayer sentiment. State laws regarding operating schools during a fiscal crisis can sometimes supersede local union agreements. For example, declining enrollments and decreased state educational funding may mandate reopening of union contractual agreements or institution of *reduction in force* (RIF). These situations can cause a legal nightmare and significant anxiety to all school stakeholders. Whenever possible, school districts should avoid these situations and plan adequately. While this may be easier said than done, alternatives to reopening a contract or an RIF may be worthwhile, such as early retirement incentive plans, hiring freezes, job transfers and consolidations, and a reduction of operating costs.

SUMMARY

The compensation of employees for a school district represents approximately 80 percent or more of the school district total budget. HR administrators need to carefully examine all the factors that motivate employees for good performance other than only relying upon pay and benefits. There are many different types of compensation programs, which include pay for performance, skills based, knowledge based, gain sharing, and merit plans that can be successfully utilized by the school board.

All these programs should be considered when improving an existing school district compensation program. The school district compensation program, however, can be one of the most important factors for recruiting, retaining, and motivating employees. Therefore the importance of remaining competitive with other school districts is a common goal for HR administrators.

CASE STUDY

You are the HR director for the Kenbar School District and have been charged with totally redesigning the teacher benefits and compensation system. The superintendent and school board have charged you to be creative in developing this new system. They are interested in a modern and leading-edge program that supports teacher accountability and motivation. One board member stated that "we don't want to give teachers raises just because they live and breathe another year—it needs to be based upon performance." Develop this comprehensive proposal with examples. Consider some of these questions in your proposal:

1. Develop a few examples of different benefits and compensation programs.
2. Outline some of the advantages and disadvantages to the programs.
3. Develop a timeframe for implementation.
4. What are some the financial ramifications to the school district for these different compensation programs?

EXERCISES AND DISCUSSION QUESTIONS

1. Many state pension programs have been underfunded, and this issue is creating fiscal nightmares. Discuss ways to address this issue.
2. List and describe at least three major federal laws impacting compensation programs.
3. List different benefit programs for teachers.
4. Many states and local school districts have encountered severe financial deficits. How can this problem be addressed through alternative employee benefit and compensation programs?
5. Some people feel that the traditional single-salary teacher schedule, based on seniority, is inherently flawed, does not provide motivation for teachers to excel, and that other forms of compensation, such as merit pay, should be considered. Discuss this issue and alternatives for providing teacher incentives.

6. The impact of reducing pay for teachers can be controversial. What are advantages and disadvantages in doing this?
7. List and describe four different types of salary structures programs.
8. How do benefits and compensation programs differ from schools?
9. Discuss the relationship between teacher pay and student performance. Does higher teacher pay relate to higher student achievement?
10. List the advantages and disadvantages of using contract employees versus full-time school district employees.

REFERENCES

Billinger, S. (2007). Principals agents? Investigating accountability in the compensation and performance of school principals. *Industrial & Labor Relations Review, 61* (1), 90–107.

Caillier, J. (2010). Paying teachers according to student achievement: Questions regarding pay-for-performance models in public education. *Clearing House, 83* (2), 58–61.

Flannery, M. (2010). How should we compensate? *NEA Today, 28* (3), 33–35.

Sawchuk, S. (2010). Merit-pay model pushed by Duncan shows no achievement edge. *Education Week, 29* (33), 1–21.

Sclafani, S. (2010). Teacher compensation around the globe. *Phi Delta Kappan, 91* (8), 38–43.

Sparks, S. (2010). Teachers pay. *Education Week, 30* (4), 384–99.

United States Bureau of Statistics (2012). Washington, DC: United States Federal Government.

World atWork. (2010). Compensation programs and practices. http://www .worldatwork.org/waw/adimLink?id=42294.

Unions and Collective Bargaining

OBJECTIVES

At the conclusion of the chapter, you will be able to:

1. List and describe the different unions in the United States (ELCC 3.1, 3.2, 3.3; ISLLC 3).
2. Describe the history of unions in the United States (ELCC 3.1; ISLLC 3).
3. Describe different advantages of unions (ELCC 3.3; ISLLC 3).
4. List and describe the various disadvantages of unions (ELCC 3.1, 3.2, 3.3; ISLLC 3).
5. Describe a typical employee union and school board collective bargaining process (ELCC 6.3; ISLLC 3).
6. List and describe various tactics and counter-tactics used in the negotiation process between the school board and union (ELCC 2.2, 6.1; ISLLC 3, 6).
7. List and describe the responsibilities of a school negotiation team (ELCC 5.1; ISLLC 3).
8. List and describe the major components of the collective bargaining agreement (ELCC 3.3, 5.1, 6.1; ISLLC 3, 6).

HISTORY OF THE LABOR MOVEMENT

The national labor movement in the United States has experienced a long and rich history (Godard, 2009). The history of organized labor can be traced back to the early 1800s. Local trade unions were formed as a result of many sweat-shop conditions that were typical during this era. Many people, especially women, worked in poor environments with long hours, sometimes sixteen hours a day with little breaks and with little pay.

The first union established was called the United Tailoresses of New York, which was formed in 1825 by a group of organized women. This early union was successful in achieving better work conditions and pay. One of the earlier large and effective unions was the Knights of Labor organized in 1869. This organization led many strikes in railroads, coalmining, and other industries as they strived to improve work conditions and pay. At times some of these strikes ended in violence and death. Perhaps the most prolific and well-known union was established in 1881 by Samuel Gompers called the Federation of Organized Trades and Labor Unions. This organization was active in the formation of trade unions, legislative matters, and child labor rights (Bahrami, Bitzan, & Leitch, 2009).

Organized labor and government agencies grew during the 1900s, although they had setbacks in membership due to the Great Depression. In 1932, the Norris-LaGuardia Anti-Injunction Act was signed into law, which specified guidelines for joining a union and was signified as a victory for the American federal labor movement. The Taft-Hartley Act of 1947 was enacted as a revision to the Wagner Act, which included additional restrictions on management and union activity, such as union membership, fair labor practices, strike provisions, and collective bargaining agreement guidelines.

Perhaps one of the most prominent labor relations agencies established by the federal government was the National Labor Relations Board (NLRB) in 1934. It still exists today and is responsible for development and administration of many labor acts and provisions governing management and union activities. However, unions have not been exempt from accusations of corruption. The Teamsters union is one of the more controversial unions and has been accused of labor racketeering and corruption activities (U.S. Bureau of Labor Statistics, 2012).

Labor unions today have experienced significant decline and only represent approximately 11 percent of the public and private workforce in the United States (Godard, 2009). Most labor unions are comprised under the parent labor organization called the American Federation of Labor–Congress of Industrial Organizations (AFL-CIO). The change in union membership has declined from a peak of approximately 30 percent to 11 percent and tends to be represented in the construction, transportation, and public employment areas. In fact, almost 40 percent of workers are unionized in public employment work. Union membership for public sector workers represents 36.2 percent as compared to the private sector workers of 6.9 percent. Workers in education and associated occupations have the highest rate of unionization at 37.1 percent.

Union membership in education tends to be more associated with states with large urban cities, such as Detroit, Chicago, and New York City, as compared to southern and southwest states. For example, Texas has only about a quarter of the number of union members as New York, even though there are almost 2 million more employees. The earnings, as reported by the Bureau of Labor Statistics, indicate that full-time union workers earned a median weekly pay of $917 as compared to the median weekly pay of $717 for nonunion workers. Variations in this statistic are impacted by occupation, geographical location, size of the organization, and industry (U.S. Bureau of Labor Statistics, 2012).

The nation's largest education organizations are the National Education Association (NEA) and American Federation of Teachers (AFT). The NEA has approximately three million members and is headquartered in Washington, DC. It also has affiliate organizations in virtually every state and employees over five hundred staff members with a budget of over 300 million dollars. The AFT was founded in Chicago in 1916, represents teachers and paraprofessionals, and is the second largest education union representing about 1.5 million members, of which about 250,000 are retired.

In 1998, a proposed merger between the two unions was rejected by the NEA. However the NEA and AFT were successful in forming a partnership in 2000 with the commitment of improving public education and mutual interests, although they both continue to operate independently. Although the NEA and AFT have a working partnership, there has been competition between them for membership over the years (Godard, 2009).

Although the unions have a right to negotiate on behalf of its members, there has been controversy in recent years. Several states have mandatory statutes that govern the rights of public employees to organize and participate in collective bargaining. Some states have taken action to eliminate the collective bargaining rights of unions. For example the State of Wisconsin, under

Governor Scott Walker, officially removed the collective bargaining rights from the majority of state public workers in 2011 and indicated that the state and local government would save 30 million dollars in the budget year. This effort was met with massive protests, opposition, and controversy.

There have been public movements in other states that follow similar patterns. In this Wisconsin ruling, a court judge ruled that the decision was unconstitutional. However the state supreme court voted four to three in favor of the governor. The right for collective bargaining by public workers undoubtedly will continue to be controversial and political.

Many school districts, especially private and charter schools, do not have union representation. Some educators believe that if a company or school district treats their people fairly, then there is no need for a union. Some potential advantages for unions include collective bargaining for increased wages and benefits, elimination of disparity in wages, job protection, and improved working conditions. However some potential disadvantages include higher costs for union membership, limited workplace flexibility, and potential reduction of individual job freedom (Koppich, 2010). Employees of any organization need to decide for themselves whether a union is best for them.

The National Labor Relations Act (NLRA) gives the right for employees to organize a union in the workplace. Employees have the right to participate in meetings, distribute union literature, wear union buttons, circulate and sign petitions, and join together for organization meetings. Also, the law protects employees from being threatened or given special promises or favors by employers. This includes but is not limited to pay increases, promotions, increased benefits, or favorable work treatment for opposing unionization (McHugh, 2007). Some of the main causes of unionization include:

- Poor working conditions,
- Favoritism or inconsistent treatment of workers,
- Employee abuse and unfair treatment,
- Inadequate benefits and wages,
- Fear of job insecurity, and
- Compromising health and safety conditions.

There are common signs that a union organization drive may be taking place. It is not unusual for union literature to be circulated, union members appear on the premises, rumors begin to circulate, and employees begin to leave the premises for union discussions and gatherings. When a union organization drive begins, management often partakes in a counter-union campaign. During this effort, management needs to be aware of the dos and don'ts of an antiunion campaign. Some of the actions that are typically allowed by management include reminding employees of the following:

- Good work conditions, wages, and benefit plans;
- Once unionized, employees may need to collaborate with union officials in order to resolve personal work issues;
- Employees do not need to talk to union organizers if they don't want to;
- Once unionized, employees will need to sign a binding contract between them and the union and must abide by union policies and regulations; and
- They will be obligated to pay union dues if unionized.

There is actually a myriad of actions that are allowed by management during a union drive and just as many actions that are not allowed according to law. For example, some of the unlawful actions by management during a union campaign include:

- Installing surveillance cameras or recording devices in union drive meeting rooms;
- Threatening employees that they will be punished if they join a union or participate in union drive activities;
- Promising employees special wages, benefits, or work conditions if they do not participate in the union drive;
- Discriminating against anyone who is interested in attending union drive activities or meetings;
- Retaliating against any employees who participate in union drive activities; and
- Broadcasting to employees that they are not to read any union drive literature, wear any union campaign buttons, and that the organization will refuse to cooperate with a union if installed.

When employees of an organization desire to form a union, they must complete a representation/certification petition with the state labor relations board. For example, the petition needs to be processed through the boards election procedures, and the petitioner needs at least 30 percent of the employees of a given unit to be certified as the exclusive collective bargaining agent for the employees. A typical form includes the name of the employer, employer representative, name of the petitioning labor organization, and affiliation if any. Other questions include if there is an existing collective bargaining agreement, are any employees currently represented by a labor organization; reason for filing a petition; number of employees proposed; and signatures of parties. If the union vote is successful, a form needs to be completed with the labor relations board as well. In addition to these activities, there are other forms for decertification petitions, charges against employers for violations, and charges against employee organization or its agents for unlawful practices, as well as notice of intent to strike form, all which need to be filed with the state and/or federal education labor relations board (Ligorner & Shengqiang, 2010).

COLLECTIVE BARGAINING AND NEGOTIATING

The process of collective bargaining can be an intense negotiating process. The process often begins with a number of activities, such as:

- Reviewing existing agreements and goals of the negotiation process;
- Establishing the time and location for negotiating and participants to be involved;
- Establishing the roles of participants, procedures for negotiating, and target dates;
- Examining past and present grievances on record by administration or union officials; and
- Agreeing to ground rules in negotiations, such as video or audio recording, policies on press releases, and impasse procedures.

Typical negotiations involve assembling the school board team, which might consist of the school board president, superintendent, and local school counsel. This team would need to conduct extensive planning and preparation, including such items as financial conditions, cost analysis, bargaining issues, work policies, roles of each member (e.g., spokespeople, observer, recorders), as well as negotiation ground rules. Likewise, the union representa-

Salary and benefits ✓	Procedures on student discipline and attendance
Teacher professional development ✓	Privacy and leave policies
Professional safety and security ✓	Class size requirements
Extracurricular duties ✓	Work conditions and hours of work
Grievance procedures ✓	Impasse procedures
Other issues in current contract	

EXHIBIT 7.1
Examples of School Board and Union Bargaining Issues

tives would outline their ground rules and bargaining issues. Exhibit 7.1 lists some typical bargaining issues between labor and management.

The negotiation process ideally should be a collaborative win-win process. All parties should demonstrate professional behavior and negotiate in good faith. Some of the positive behaviors in negotiating include:

- Respecting all members and listening to their concerns,
- Controlling emotions and remaining calm,
- Taking good notes,
- Staying alert and being a good participant,
- Keeping on the subject and not getting off on tangents,
- Being open-minded and cooperative, and
- Avoiding premature judgments and distractions, such as using smart-phones and cell phones

During the negotiation process, it is not unusual that different tactics and counter-tactics will occur. Exhibit 7.2 lists examples of negotiating tactics.

While there are many tactics that can be utilized during the negotiating process, it is important to recognize that there are just as many counter-tactics to these tactics. For example, if one is presented with the "*What if*" question, the other party might counter this tactic by ignoring the statement and suggesting alternative what-ifs as well. The use of *fait accompli* is an attempt to bring quick closure and agreement to negotiations. However, the other party should use patience and perhaps confront the other party as instigating a ploy to discourage this type of behavior. When faced with the *quick deal* the party should resist the tendency to give in and perhaps resort to the *forbearance* tactic. Often requesting additional information and being patient may allow the party to discover other insightful information.

Tactic	Description
Emotional tantrum	Exhibiting strong emotions in an attempt to gain control over the other party.
Fait accompli	Presenting a final offer (accomplished fact) in an attempt to bring closure to the negotiations.
Take it or leave it	Making a final offer to the other party in order to close the negotiations.
Good guy–bad guy	Using a combination of a hostile negotiator and a friendly negotiator to gain a competitive advantage.
What if	Asking a flurry of questions in order to pry information from the other party.
Dumb is smart—smart is dumb	Asking dumb questions in order to gain information from the other party that might not otherwise be obtained.
The expert	Bringing in expert testimony or facts and data to convince the other party of your position.
Emotional insulation	Being purposely silent and not responding to create uncomfortable feelings in the other party and gain information.
Deadlock	Playing brinksmanship to increase the party's power and strength and encourage concessions from the other party.

EXHIBIT 7.2
Examples of Negotiation Tactics and Descriptions

Other tactics that can help a party during negotiations include knowing the facts, figures, and all information that is being negotiated; procedural laws; guidelines and standards; having total commitment for the negotiating process; becoming as knowledgeable as possible about the process and bargaining issues; taking risks; and developing one's negotiating skills. During the negotiating process, it is good to keep in mind that human beings are social creatures and have similar feelings and aspirations. People generally want to be listened to, treated respectfully, given accurate information in good faith, and avoid uncertainty. Understanding these natural human feelings and behaviors can benefit the negotiator during the collective bargaining process.

Every lead negotiator has a style unique to him or her. Exhibit 7.3 lists several styles of negotiating. Understanding the different styles of negotiating can be helpful during the negotiation process. For example, Warschaw (1980) describes six specific negotiating styles, which include *jungle fighters*, *dictators*, *silhouettes*, *big mama/big daddy*, *soothers*, and *win-win negotiators*. The ideal negotiating style is the win-win negotiator. This person is objective,

Negotiating Style	Characteristics
Jungle Fighters	Creative and charismatic, but demeaning and aggressive
Dictators	Assertive, analytical, and shrewd, but rigid, demanding, and judgmental
Silhouettes	Discrete, loyal, and tenacious, but reclusive, evasive, and uncommunicative
Big Mama/Big Daddy	Caring, nurturing, supporting, and gracious, but manipulative, devious, nonrevealing, and overprotective
Soothers	Helpful, attentive, and appreciative, but anxious, indecisive, and evasive
Win-Win Negotiators	Objective, nonjudgmental, specific, and open, and ideally has no liabilities

EXHIBIT 7.3
Negotiation Styles
Source: Warschaw (1980).

nonjudgmental, motivated for collaborative negotiations, and sensitive and open during the process. Ideally this style lacks any liabilities. Each of the other styles of negotiating has assets and liabilities, as listed in exhibit 7.3. By becoming aware of one's own style of negotiating and the style of the other party, striving to become the win-win negotiator can help in achieving a successful negotiation.

Another popular theory of negotiations is called the *principled negotiations model*. This model has been described in the book *Getting to Yes* (Ury & Fisher, 1981). In this model, the authors outline several valuable principles and strategies for reaching agreement in the negotiation process. Examples of these principles include "goal as agreement, not victory"; "be soft on people and hard on the problem"; "accept one-sided losses to reach agreement"; and "view participants as friends versus adversaries" (Ury & Fisher, 1981). This theory of negotiation supports the concept of collaborative negotiations and can serve to help reach consensus.

Another theory that can be helpful in the negotiation process is *emotional intelligence*. Effective negotiators have qualities such as intelligence, ability to persuade people, and emotional intelligence. Emotions play a significant part in the negotiation process. Negotiators can be very intelligent, however if they lack the emotional skills to deal with people, they might likely give concessions. Goldman (1995) articulates five basic competencies necessary for emotionally intelligent people: *self-awareness*, *self-regulation*, *self-motivation*, *empathy*, and *effective relationships*. Self-awareness describes the degree to which a negotiator understands his or her personal feelings (e.g., anger, anxiety, and avoidance) and how these feelings affect one's self during negotiations. If a person has a high degree of self-awareness, he or she understands what triggers these emotions in him- or herself. The first step to being emotionally intelligent is to understand what sets off one's emotions so that one can be aware of them during the bargaining process. There have been intellectually capable people, however they lack the ability to control their emotions. Emotions drive decision making and may produce poor results.

The competency of self-regulation describes a person's ability to monitor his or her emotional feelings and be able to regulate them. Once feelings are triggered, the person is then able to employ necessary skills to control negative behaviors and regulate them in a most productive manner. This may be done through self-talk and self-control. For example, during the negotiating process, if the other party elicits a trigger that produces an emotional reaction, an effective negotiator becomes aware of this trigger and is able to self-regulate this emotion so that he or she does not become distracted.

Self-motivation is the third competency, which describes a person's ability to direct his or her feelings toward a constructive purpose. All negotiators experience success and failures during the bargaining process. When a person is able to recognize failures, be realistic, and is able to grow and learn from these mistakes, this suggests competence in this self-motivational level. The negotiator's ability to discern between important bargaining issues and unimportant issues can be critical in this stage. Simply put, some bargaining issues are more important than others, and during the negotiation process, concession making is critical.

The empathy competency is the fourth level, which describes a person's ability to not only recognize and regulate his or her emotions but also be able to understand how these emotions affect other people. In this stage, the person is able to see from another party's perspective and be aware of vulnerabilities.

The last level of emotional intelligence is that of effective relationships. Effective negotiators who are emotionally intelligent must be able to create a humanistic bargaining environment. Essentially, at this stage, the negotiator is able to separate his or her ego from the bargaining issues. In this way the negotiator can be more objective in dealing with the other party. Developing skills in each of these five competencies can help a negotiator become more successful during the bargaining process.

During the negotiating process, the negotiator also needs to develop good communication skills. There are several strategies that can be utilized during the negotiation process. For example, the skilled negotiator might utilize the technique of *paraphrasing*. *Paraphrasing* means to repeat back to the other party in the negotiator's own words what was stated. This helps to reinforce the point that the negotiator is listening to the other party and ensure that the message was understood.

The use of *restatement* is another technique that can be used. *Restatement* means that the negotiator repeats verbatim the other party's statement in an effort to encourage the party to continue talking. The use of *open-ended* and *closed-ended questions* can also be a valuable technique. Open-ended questions cannot be answered by a simple "yes" or "no" and therefore encourages the other party to continue talking. Open-ended questions usually involve words such as *who, what, where, when,* and *how*. The use of open-ended questions encourages the seeking of additional facts and information. Closed-ended questions can be effectively used when the negotiator simply wants to obtain and "yes" or "no" answer. A simple phrase can yield a great bit of information and expedite the negotiation discussion over bargaining issues.

Silence can be a powerful technique when negotiating between two parties. When faced with silence, people will often talk. Using moments of silence in a skillful manner by the negotiator can sometimes produce valuable information by allowing the other party to open up discussion and provide information. Silence can also demonstrate that the negotiator is genuinely willing to listen to the other party's concern.

The use of *expanders* is a technique of stating simple comments, such as "go on," "I understand," and "I see." Expanders encourage the other party to continue talking, and they have a reinforcing effect in establishing a negotiating dialog.

The concept of *concession making* is a critical one during the negotiation process. Good negotiators always allow themselves to negotiate. Some strategies for concession-making include:

- Ask the other party to reveal their demands first.
- Regulate and record all concession making.
- Seek opinions prior to agreeing to a concession.
- Try to obtain a concession from the other party for every concession given.

- Recognize that concessions are often given at the last minute or deadline for negotiation.

There are many things that can go wrong during a negotiation process, and there are often very high stakes on the table. Not only is there a need to obtain agreement from the other party, but also generally the lead negotiators need to gain approval from their own constituents (e.g., school board or union members). Unfortunately not all negotiations end amicably.

When negotiations reach an impasse, there are federal and state guidelines for proceeding. It is always beneficial for parties to emphasize the benefits for reaching agreement as well as the potential ill effects. In attempting to reach agreement, parties can encourage settlement by discussing the details of the agreement, taking a break, changing the negotiators if deadlock occurs, and maintaining a positive attitude. Sometimes experienced negotiators like to compare the current negotiating process with past negotiating sessions. In this way the negotiator attempts to bring about consensus and agreement to the bargaining issues (McHugh, 2007).

REACHING AN IMPASSE

If an impasse is encountered, some of the common remedies include the use of *mediation* and *arbitration*. Mediation involves securing a mediator to act as a facilitator to attempt to broker agreement between the two parties. Generally this process is not binding and is only an attempt to persuade each party to resolve the bargaining issues. Arbitration is similar to mediation but generally involves securing a third-party arbitrator who will review the overall bargaining issues and render a decision that becomes binding (Maciejewski, 2007)

Often when agreement is reached between the two parties, a ratification vote by the members and the board is necessary. If both parties are able to approve the agreement with their constituents, the agreement is consummated. It is not unusual for one of the parties not to achieve agreement, and they need to go back to the bargaining table for additional rounds of negotiation. It should be noted that the arbitration could be voluntary or compulsory.

Some states utilize compulsory arbitration as determined by state law. Other ways to resolve negotiation disputes can be done through the use of the Federal Mediation Conciliation Service (FMCS). This is an agency created by the federal government with the primary goal of promoting labor-management collaboration (Martinez-Pecino, Jaca, Medina, & Euwema, 2008). The office of this agency is located in Washington, DC, and it contains a list of many arbitrators who are available throughout the country.

The FMCS was created in 1947, is headquartered in Washington, DC, and has more than seventy field offices. FMCS provides both mediators and arbitrators. When a mediator is used, some of the strategies they provide include reestablishing negotiation ground rules, clarifying issues and disputes, helping parties define problems, keeping the negotiation process moving along, promoting communications and exchange of information, and managing conflict (Federal Mediation Conciliation Service, 2011). In addition, FMCS provides a number of different services, such as creating annual reports, providing audits of financial statements, performance and accountability reports, annual employee surveys, and congressional matters relevant to labor-management collective bargaining (Lawson, 2011).

Unfortunately, if labor-management negotiations break down, then a strike may occur. A strike is one of the final and deadliest weapons in the union's arsenal that can be used against a board of education. However, strikes come with a price and often have detriment to student learning, employee loss of pay, disruption in the workplace, community dissatisfaction, and animosity among all school stakeholders. Generally the state education labor relations board requires a *notice of intent to strike* for union bargaining units. Therefore, the use of the strike provision should be a last resort.

Unions often use the strike as a last resort to gain concessions and reach agreement from the school board. It is possible by law that, when employees participate in a strike, they may be eligible for termination by the school board for failure to carry out contractual responsibilities. A specialized type of strike is called the "wildcat" strike. This is a strike that is unauthorized by state legislation and serves the intention of creating a work stoppage by union employees. Regardless if the strike is authorized or not, it may or may not be announced by union officials prior to striking. Tactical advantages for making an announcement or not can be determined by union leadership.

SUMMARY

The collective bargaining process is one of critical importance to a school district. The negotiation process should not be done by unskilled representatives. Skillful negotiators need to thoroughly understand compensation contracts, working conditions, tactics of negotiations, federal and state laws, and the psychology of human interactions. All these areas can contribute to the success during the collective bargaining process. However, if both parties cannot reach agreement, outside facilitators may need to be secured. Mediators and arbitrators are commonly used to assist in these matters. Both are considered third-party facilitators.

Mediation is generally not binding and serves to help the parties reach agreement, while arbitration can either be voluntary or involuntary but often is considered binding in nature. The collective bargaining process should be approached by all parties with good-faith intentions. When both parties utilize a win-win collaborative negotiation process, they are more likely to reach an amicable agreement that best services all stakeholders of the school district.

CASE STUDY

You are the human resources director for the Johnsonville School District and have been charged with leading the upcoming school board union negotiations. The former negotiations between union and management have not gone well. The union has taken a very aggressive and confrontational approach to negotiations. They have invested significant money and outside legal counsel and consultants in an attempt to gain the best contract they can. The school board is under a lot of pressure to deal with the union and create a more cooperative relationship. In preparation for the upcoming negotiation, the school board has requested that you prepare the following:

1. Develop a list of the top six or so bargaining issues that you want to pursue.
2. Create a list of six or so anticipated tactics that may be used against you, and develop counter-tactics for each of them.
3. Develop a list of several professional behaviors that you feel are conducive for collaborative negotiations.
4. Develop a list of six or more ground rules for undertaking the negotiation process.

EXERCISES AND DISCUSSION QUESTIONS

1. Describe the history of unions in the United States.
2. Describe the impact of the emergence of teacher unions in the United States.

3. Media coverage of state and municipal opposition to union bargaining has caused controversy in this country and the feeling that unions may be exhibiting too much power and influence, while others feel that unions should have the right to bargain. Discuss this issue and various approaches for resolving this sentiment.

4. Many states and local school districts have encountered severe financial deficits and cannot continue to offer educational programs and extracurricular activities. This situation has also, in some cases, caused hardship for local taxpayers. Discuss ways to deal with this situation.

5. List different teacher union organizations and the history to attempt to merge these organizations into one large union organization. What are the drawbacks to this?

6. The impact of collective bargaining on education has created an adversarial relationship between state government and union members, such as the case in the State of Wisconsin. Discuss the ramifications of these situations, and provide opinions on addressing this issue.

7. List different unions for classified staff of school districts in the United States.

8. With the increase of charter and private schools, many of these schools do not have collective bargaining or union representation as compared to many public schools. Discuss the fiscal and human resource advantages and disadvantages of these structures and potential impact on student learning.

9. The State of Wisconsin legislation eliminated the collective bargaining rights of some public workers with the state. List the advantages and disadvantages in this decision.

10. List the advantages and disadvantages for having union representation for teachers in a school district.

REFERENCES

Bahrami, B., Bitzan, J., & Leitch, J. (2009). Union worker wage effect in the public sector. *Journal of Labor Research, 30* (1), 35–51.

Federal Mediation and Conciliation Service. (2011). www.fmcs.gov.

Godard, J. (2009). The exceptional decline of the American labor movement. *Industrial & Labor Relations Review, 63* (1), 82–108.

Goleman, D. (1995). *Emotional intelligence.* New York: Bantam Books.

Koppich, J. (2010). Teacher unions and new forms of teacher compensation. *Phi Delta Kappan, 91* (8), 22–26.

Lawson, N. (2011). Is collective bargaining Pareto efficient? A survey of the literature. *Journal of Labor Research, 32* (3), 282–304.

Ligorner, K., & Shengqiang, L. T. (2010). Unionization and collective bargaining: New tools for social harmony. *China Business Review, 37* (6), 28–31.

Maciejewski, J. (2007). Broadening collective bargaining. *District Administration, 43* (7), 34–39.

Martinez-Pecino, R., Jaca, L. M., Medina, F. J., & Euwema, M. (2008). Effectiveness of mediation strategies in collective bargaining. *Industrial Relations: A Journal of Economy and Society, 47* (3), 480–95.

McHugh, P. (2007). Collective bargaining context and worker attitudes: Comparing team and traditional work systems. *Journal of Labor Research, 28* (4), 697–713.

U.S. Bureau of Labor Statistics. (2012). Washington, DC: U.S. Federal Government.

Ury, L., & Fisher, R. (1981). *Getting to yes: Negotiating without giving in.* New York: Penguin.

Warschaw, T. (1980). *Winning by negotiations.* New York: McGraw-Hill.

8

Managing Human Resources

OBJECTIVES

At the conclusion of this chapter, you will be able to:

1. Understand the relationship between student achievement and allocating personnel resources (ELCC 3.3; ISLCC 3).
2. Understand what education resources are (ELCC 4.3; ISLLC 4).
3. Articulate strategies for allocating personnel resources for higher performance and productivity (ELCC 3.3, 4.3; ISLLC 3, 4).
4. Describe the core and noncore functions of a school (ELCC 3.2; ISLLC 3).
5. Understand various approaches to identifying efficiencies in a school or school district (ELCC 3.3; ISLLC 3).
6. Understand the role of position control in a school district (ELCC 3.3; ISLLC 3).
7. Describe the role of technology as it relates to human resources (ELCC 3.3; ISLLC 3).

WHAT ARE EDUCATIONAL RESOURCES?

Public school leaders across the country appear to be nearing consensus about the necessary characteristics of successful schools. Class size, an advanced college preparatory curriculum, teacher professional development, and differentiated instruction are key factors in helping all students learn (Newstead, Saxton, & Colby, 2008). However, implementing these programs is not a cost-neutral endeavor. On the other hand, authors like Stephen Brill note that "if school systems stopped adhering to class size limits now that we know that class size counts less than the quality of the teacher in front of the class," they could invest more in teacher salaries (Brill, 2011).

Educational resources come in many forms. Tying those resources to standards and student outcomes is important not only to have an effective program but an efficient one. What is equally important is how those resources are targeted within a state, school district, and school building. Exhibit 8.1 shows the pupil–teacher ratio for elementary and secondary schools from 1970 through 2009. Note that the overall ratio has dropped approximately seven students per teacher during this time period.

Schools tend to reallocate funds differently from other organizations due to funding constraints, union contracts, and other factors. School educators can define their priorities, but that does not guarantee that the funds can or will be distributed to those areas. In order to assure a proper reallocation of resources, the principal should be the responsible party that leads a team in researching the trouble areas of the school to determine whether it is possible for the reallocation. The Center for Comprehensive School Reform and Improvement (2009) observes that

> the complexity of the task of allocating resources within a school is directly related to the quantity and type of resources available for reallocation. It is easier to allocate money than it is to reallocate, which requires taking hold from one area of the school to provide in another. Before starting the process, school leaders should examine the situation in which they will be working to determine if the context is conducive to school-level resource allocation. Addressing problems in this area in advance is helpful because changes in school district resource allocation and accountability processes may be needed before the work can proceed.

By following this procedure, the school leader can make better decisions on how and what should be reallocated with documented support through the research process to reduce possible school inequities.

ALLOCATING RESOURCES FOR HIGHER PERFORMANCE AND PRODUCTIVITY

School administrators are constantly challenged to meet the academic and socializing goals for the students they educate. Whereas private businesses seek

Year	Teachers		Enrollment		Pupil–Teacher Ratio	
	Public	Private	Public	Private	Public	Private
1970	2,059	233	45,894	5,363	22.3	23.0
1975	2,198	255	44,819	5,000	20.4	19.6
1980	2,184	301	40,877	5,331	18.7	17.7
1984	2,168	340	39,208	5,700	18.1	16.8
1985	2,206	343	39,442	5,557	17.9	16.2
1986	2,244	348	39,753	5,452	17.7	15.7
1987	2,279	352	40,008	5,479	17.6	15.6
1988	2,323	345	40,189	5,242	17.3	15.2
1989	2,357	356	40,543	5,198	17.2	15.7
1990	2,388	361	41,217	5,234	17.2	15.6
1991	2,432	365	42,047	5,681	17.3	15.6
1992	2,459	368	42,823	5,677	17.4	15.4
1993	2,504	370	43,465	5,668	17.4	15.3
1994[1]	2,552	373	44,111	5,787	17.3	15.5
1995	2,598	376	44,840	5,918	17.3	15.7
1996[1]	2,667	384	45,611	5,933	17.1	15.5
1997	2,746	391	46,127	5,944	16.8	15.2
1998[1]	2,830	400	46,539	5,988	16.4	15.0
1999	2,911	408	46,857	6,018	16.1	14.7
2000[1]	2,941	424	47,204	6,169	16.0	14.5
2001	3,000	441	47,672	6,320	15.9	14.3
2002[1]	3,034	442	48,183	6,220	15.9	14.1
2003	3,049	441	48,540	6,099	15.9	13.8
2004[1]	3,091	445	48,795	6,087	15.8	13.7
2005	3,143	450	49,113	6,073	15.6	13.5
2006[1]	3,166	456	49,316	5,991	15.6	13.2
2007	3,178	456	49,293	5,910	15.5	13.0
2008[1]	3,219	455	49,266	5,969	15.3	13.1
2009[2]	3,161	457	49,312	5,970	15.6	13.1

[1]Private school numbers are estimated based on data from the Private School Universe Survey.

[2]Projection.

EXHIBIT 8.1
Elementary and Secondary Schools—Teachers, Enrollment, and Pupil–Teacher Ratio, 1970 to 2009. [In thousands (2,292 represents 2,292,000), except ratios. As of fall each year. Dates are for full-time equivalent teachers. Based on surveys of state education agencies and private schools; see resource for details.]

Source: U.S. Census Bureau. U.S. National Center for Education Statistics (2012). Digest of Education Statistics, annual, and Projections of Educational Statistics. See also www.nces.ed.gov/annuals.

to minimize overhead and increase profits, public schools tend to maximize the utilization of budgets in support of increasing achievement. In economically challenged times, businesses reduce expenses and increase efficiency to stay in business and attempt to stay profitable. For businesses, productivity is the key. School districts are not used to thinking of productivity in the same terms as private businesses. Schools tend to think of efficiency as simply making cuts to balance their budgets. However, making certain cuts can be counterproductive. Basically, there are only three methods of balancing a school budget: cut spending, increase revenues, or a combination of both (Wong & Casing, 2010).

Unfortunately for most public school districts, the only viable alternative is to cut spending. Spending is the only thing a school district has total control over. So with these challenges, how do we allocate resources for higher performance and productivity in public schools? As Daggett (2009) notes, school districts need to focus "resources and accountability around specific tools, strategies, professional development, procedures, and policies that can be documented to improve student performance" (p. 15). He goes on to state that this is a subtle change from what currently exists—it shifts the focus from inputs (programs) to outputs (student performance). Education Resource Strategies, Inc., has developed five strategies to help low-performing schools improve their chances for success (Baroody, 2011). Those strategies are:

1. Understand what each school needs.
2. Quantify what each school gets and how it is used.
3. Invest in the most important changes first.
4. Customize the strategy to the school.
5. Change the district, not just the school.

Increasing performance and productivity are dependent on many variables. The key to implementing any plan is to first identify the parameters, needs, and options available. This process should be done in collaboration with staff, taxpayers, and other stakeholders. The second step is to identify the strategies that are available for achieving the outcomes. Outcomes include not only those related to the academic achievement of students but also the fiscal health of the organization. Both these outcomes directly affect human resource allocations and planning.

Class size is probably the biggest driver of educational resources. In a small elementary school with only two sections of each grade level, losing two students per grade probably doesn't mean you're going to have any significant savings. On the other hand, in a large school with multiple sections, you may find that you can increase class size by a few students, not affect achievement, and realize staffing reductions and savings. Again, all of this is affected by the composition of the class. In the final analysis, most districts, when faced with budget reductions, will closely guard class sizes as opposed to other nonessential support services.

Like most bureaucracies, schools and school districts tend to maintain programs already in existence and have difficulty eliminating those that no longer are effective. Demographics change as well as best practices and student needs. Confirming educational needs is important in that it forces organizations to reevaluate programs in light of student outcomes. The result of such a process is that resources can be reallocated and realigned to promote student achievement in a productive and efficient manner.

Care should be exercised to comply with all legal requirements. Most categorical programs such as special education, response to intervention (RTI), and bilingual programs have specific requirements set by the state. RTI, which focuses on research-based interventions and instruction for general education students, has been adopted by a growing number of states in America (Zirkel, 2011). RTI, which focuses primarily on reading improvement, may hold the promise of reducing costs by implementing early interventions.

There are several strategies to confirm an organization's current instructional needs. Among these is reviewing information that will shed light on which practices, programs, and policies have been effective and produced measurable improvements in student achievement and outcomes. Simply put, invest in what works. This is especially important in times of limited educational resources. Shifting resources from less-effective to more-effective programs and strategies will most likely result in the least amount of harm to students.

Part of the process of confirming educational needs requires that new courses, programs, and instructional strategies contain a fiscal analysis or business plan. Educators need to commit the organization to evaluating new initiatives from both an instructional and fiscal basis. Also, educators need to determine if there is evidence that the results achieved are cost effective or if the resources designated for the new initiative could be better spent on investing in current programs and services. Often educators just look at the cost of staff and textbooks. A better approach would be to include all costs: staff, benefits, professional development, supplies, textbooks, equipment, digital materials, facilities, and so on. How many students will the initiative serve? Will there be a need for indirect resources, such as counselors, media specialists, technologists, and so on.

Schools and school districts can utilize a more structured and systematic approach to confirming instructional needs (Cook, 1979). The *educational program review technique* (EPRT) provides school districts with a means of comparing programs and functions within their system on several levels— priority, impact on achievement, and cost (Fox & Prombo, 2010). How does EPRT work? Basically it involves reviewing and evaluating programs on their effectiveness. Program plans are submitted at various funding levels outlining expected outcomes, activities, and evaluation techniques at each level. In the case of Community Unit School District 300 in Illinois, those levels are about a 10 percent reduction, the status quo, and an increase of about 10 percent in allocated financial resources. (Fox & Prombo, 2010). Once all the data is acquired, programs are then ranked based on whether they should be reduced, stay the same, or receive more resources.

The primary purpose of schools and school systems is to educate children. In accomplishing that purpose, a number of services are necessary that have nothing to do with student achievement or outcomes. Those services could be referred to as noncore functions of the school as opposed to the core competencies of academic preparation. In private industry, if a function is not generating a profit, it is usually considered a noncore function, and organizations seek the most efficient ways of providing the service. In schools and school districts, the noncore functions might include transporting students, custodial and maintenance services, food service, security, and other similar auxiliary services.

Not all states allow for the outsourcing of these services or have passed stringent rules protecting work done by union employees from arbitrarily being outsourced. However, in states where outsourcing is legal, it can lead to substantial savings in these noncore functions. Whether these services are provided internally or externally, they should be reviewed periodically to ensure they are being provided in the most efficient and cost-effective manner. Schools and school districts need to adopt an entrepreneurial mindset in this regard. They need to ask four key questions (Schilling, 2006):

1. Why am I doing this?
2. If I don't do this, what's the consequence?

3. Can somebody else do it better?
4. Is it a core competency?

The key to managing staff efficiently and effectively is to have an effective position control system. Simply, a position control system defines every position within an organization, attaches every employee to a specific position, and then tracks all costs associated with these positions, including vacancies. Why is this important? Approximately 75 to 85 percent of all school district expenditures are associated with human resources costs—salary and benefits (Beyne & Bedford, 2009). Position control system can help improve fiscal efficiency and serve to:

- Assist with staff planning and hiring, budgetary control, and position monitoring;
- Ensure staff are only assigned to authorized positions;
- Eliminate payments to staff that are not authorized in the budget; and
- Provide accountability by department and activity for positions hired, maintained, and funded.

An effective position control system creates checks and balances between personnel decisions and budgets. It ensures the position is not only authorized but is available, has funding, and is assigned to the correct account. Position control systems are especially useful tools in human resource forecasting. Defining a position includes not only compensation but also benefits, work week/year, leave entitlements, and other contractual benefits.

Process mapping is another strategy that can be used to streamline operations and increase efficiency. A process map defines how an organization performs work, the steps and sequence involved, who is responsible for each step, and how various groups interact (Beyne & Bedford, 2011). Exhibit 8.2 shows an example of a process map for a school district business function.

Exhibit 8.3 shows the purchasing process after it was revised. Notice how many fewer steps there are in the process. This results in both efficiency and productivity gains by just changing how things are done. In other words, the organization may need fewer staff to perform the tasks, or the time saved may be repurposed for other tasks.

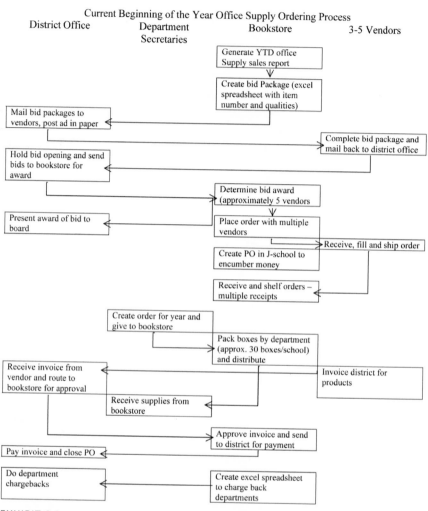

Current Beginning of the Year Office Supply Ordering Process

District Office	Department Secretaries	Bookstore	3-5 Vendors

Generate YTD office Supply sales report

Create bid Package (excel spreadsheet with item number and qualities)

Mail bid packages to vendors, post ad in paper

Complete bid package and mail back to district office

Hold bid opening and send bids to bookstore for award

Determine bid award (approximately 5 vendors

Present award of bid to board

Place order with multiple vendors

Receive, fill and ship order

Create PO in J-school to encumber money

Receive and shelf orders – multiple receipts

Create order for year and give to bookstore

Pack boxes by department (approx. 30 boxes/school) and distribute

Receive invoice from vendor and route to bookstore for approval

Invoice district for products

Receive supplies from bookstore

Approve invoice and send to district for payment

Pay invoice and close PO

Do department chargebacks

Create excel spreadsheet to charge back departments

EXHIBIT 8.2.
Example of Process Mapping

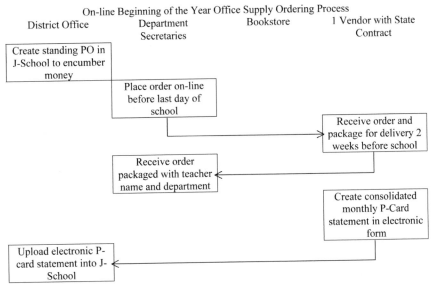

EXHIBIT 8.3.
Example of a Final Process Map for Purchasing

Process mapping can also be useful to:

1. Document and map existing human practices, including, but not limited to, hiring and replacing positions, changing hours and/or funding of positions, and payroll-related issues;

2. Outline key practices that may hinder internal workflow, data-based decision making, authorization, and management of personnel-related activities; and

3. Provide recommendations for minimizing or eliminating duplicate activities, streamlining work functions, minimizing errors, enhancing productivity, and eliminating non-value-added activity (e.g., multiple recording of data).

Common sense would tell us that we should only pay for what we need. Practically, however, this is not always the case. Many school districts consider a full-time employee to be 8 hours per day for 260 days, or 2,080 hours per year. The following shows how just a small change in those contracts can result in a substantial savings:

BEFORE: The district has 100 secretaries working 8 hours per day for 260 days. Those secretaries are entitled to an average of 15 holidays and 10 days of vacation. They are scheduled for winter and spring break. The average salary is $30,000 per year. Total cost to the school district: $30,000 × 100 = $3,000,000.

AFTER: The district identifies a core of 20 secretarial positions that need to work full-time over the winter and spring breaks and during the summer. For the remaining positions, the district eliminates work over the winter break (10 days) and spring break (5 days), and during the summer, these positions only work a 4-day work week for 8 weeks (8 days). The result is that staff will work only when they are needed. The district can also possibly negotiate or reduce the amount of vacation time since the staff will be off the equivalent of about 5 weeks. Furthermore, the district could implement the change as positions open. Total cost to the school district after changes: $30,000 × 20 = $600,000, plus $27,346 × 80 = $2,187,680, for a total of $2,787,680—an annual savings of $212,320, or 7 percent.

Human resource audits can be performed internally or with the help of an outside consulting firm. A human resource audit can be used to review specific practices or simply define positions and compensation levels. A full personnel or human resource audit would include identifying personnel demographics, including number of positions, salary and tenure, compliance with personnel recordkeeping, compliance with federal and state laws, employment and recruiting practices, evaluation processes, and job descriptions. As noted previously, human resource audits can also be used to identify processes, practices, and compensation levels. When used in this manner, this audit can result in efficiencies through workflow analysis and alignment of positions and compensation. The following example is one such approach to conducting this type of audit for a clerical staff:

- Develop a bank of questions (tasks) for the clerical staff and department focus groups to procure feedback. Focus groups would include administrators only, clerical staff only, and cross-sectional groups that would include both administrative and clerical staff. Examples of questions would include:

- What percentage of the time do you spend interacting with students each day? Who are your customers? What tasks performed by administrators could be performed by clerical staff?
- Identify and distribute a list of tasks to all staff, and ask them to identify the frequency the tasks are performed (daily, weekly, monthly, etc.).
- Identify the appropriate job classifications used by the U.S. Department of Labor as opposed to traditional school categories. This allows for regional, state, and national comparisons as well as standardized categories and job descriptions. For a clerical staff, the categories might include executive secretaries and administrative assistants, secretaries, bookkeeping, accounting and audit clerks, and receptionist and information clerks (Bureau of Labor Statistics, U.S. Department of Labor, 2012).

What might be a typical result of such an analysis? Surveying one hundred clerical staff, a district may find out that department secretaries really spend most of their day as receptionists and information clerks, which would include answering phones, greeting visitors, responding to inquiries from the public, and so forth.

USING TECHNOLOGY TO MANAGE HUMAN RESOURCES

Technology can play a significant role in increasing productivity at every level of the education system. Human resource management is no exception. From a human resources perspective, technology should assist with the following activities:

- Employee Information: managing, maintaining, reporting;
- Position Control: tracking, managing, and authorizing district positions and related budget impacts;
- Job Assignments: process for tracking, monitoring, and managing individual employee job assignments and related site/location, full-time equivalency, work calendars, and funding accounts;
- Compensation Details: process for employee salary placement (linkage to salary schedules and special compensation, such as stipends and/or longevity pay;
- Certificates/Credentials: process to track teacher certification information;

- No Child Left Behind (NCLB): process to document highly qualified teachers and NCLB compliance;
- Professional Growth: tracking of educational course information by employee, including semester hours/units;
- Emergency Contacts: process to update and maintain employees' emergency contact information (integration potential with current system and, if no current system, documentation of process to smooth transition);
- Health and Welfare Benefits: process for managing and tracking employee health benefits, including plan, policy, and associated premiums;
- Evaluations: process for tracking employee evaluation dates and outcomes;
- Substitute Assignments: process for managing and tracking various substitute assignments, as well as linkages to rate of pay for each assignment;
- Service History: process of historical accounting of all previous job assignment history and associated service credit tracking; and
- Reporting: access to timely, accurate, and comprehensive employee data.

In addition, there a number of activities for which there may be shared responsibility with the school districts business office. Those activities include processes to:

- Record and manage employee attendance and/or absence transactions by attendance period;
- Manage employee leave balances, such as sick leave, vacation, and personal necessity;
- Account for substitute work and associated pay;
- Authorize and post all employee leave associated with conferences or other professional development and related funding;
- Authorize and post employee extra duty activity, pay, overtime, and stipend compensation; and
- Manage all compensation-related transactions by pay period.

Escalating costs, inadequate or missing authorizations, missing controls, and redundant processes are all reasons for implementing comprehensive *human resource software*. Human resource software should be dynamic, providing real-time data. It should be date driven. When an event such as a retirement or vacancy is known, it should be recorded in the system. Likewise, administrators should be able to ascertain vacancies, positions, absences, and contractual obligations on any given day, whether in the past or future. This is also crucial for reporting personnel positions and costs to boards of education and the public.

The process of obtaining an adequate human resource software system can be intimidating. Ideally, the software would be fully integrated with other software, such as finance and business. As noted earlier, there are some key features that no software system should be without. Those include real-time process, date-driven data, and position control. Furthermore, employees should have the ability to access the system for basic information. This both saves staff time and provides a layer of transparency with regard to employee information. Exhibit 8.4 is a checklist of the main features that should be considered when selecting a human resources software system.

SHARED SERVICES

Another strategy that schools and school districts can utilize is *shared services*. This can have a direct or indirect impact on personnel needs. Consolidating services has resulted in cost savings and efficiencies in many states. Intergovernmental agreements for the delivery of low-incidence special education students and vocational education cooperatives are also common. In some states, investment pools, cooperative bidding, state purchasing cooperatives, and shared fiscal services have also resulted in savings. Small school districts in particular that have limited purchasing power, small staffs, and fewer funds to invest are most likely to be the biggest beneficiaries of cooperative or shared services ventures. Following is a list of possible shared services in which school districts may engage that may impact human resource planning:

- Curriculum planning,
- Custodial services,
- Employee benefits,
- Food services,
- Staff recruitment,
- Professional development,
- Purchasing and procurement,
- Special education,
- Technology services,
- Transportation services, and
- Vocational education.

The Technology

Who hosts? __ The district (self-hosted) __ The vendor ___ Someone else (county, township)

If hosted by the vendor (i.e., SaaS—Software as a Service), what are you looking for? (check all that might apply)

__ Experience
__ Performance record
__ Failover site
__ Backup timing
__ Frequency of upgrades
__ Capacity of servers
__ District data escrow (What if the vendor goes out of business?)
__ Information security (physical and network)

If self-hosted (district provides the hosting), what do you need to know? (check all that might apply)

__ Cost of staff to maintain
__ Server capacity
__ Staff availability and costs of overtime
__ Failover site
__ Data backup
__ Equipment upgrades
__ Keeper of the data
__ Information security (physical and network)

What is the technology?
__ Web-browser-based
__ Remote desktop / 2x / Citrix-based—virtual desktop
__ Silverlight
__ HTML5

How often are releases done? ___
Are releases extra charges? ___

History of Releases

What does the district need?
__ Financial/Payroll
__ Human resources/Position control
__ Budgeting driven from personnel costs
__ Status change capabilities for tracking
__ Accountability and authorization for all timesheet activity
__ Student information system
__ Data warehouse
__ Integrated sub calling
__ Integrated applicant tracking
__ Everything integrated: One vendor fits all
__ Best-practices-only approach with ability to integrate where needed with other applications

What Should Pricing Include (check all that apply)?

__ New releases
__ Training during implementation
__ Training updates (webinars) after implementation
__ Customer service support
__ Implementation

__ All data imports and exports
__ Configurations (vendor will set limits)
__ Flat annual fee for __ years
__ Fixed range estimate on renewal fee for contract
__ Pricing in one place visible! No hidden fees: Know the exact price tag at purchase

Services and Support: Things to Ask (check all that apply)
__ Hours of operation and availability
__ Trained professionals to meet the need
__ User support request system
__ Issue escalation process
__ Dedicated primary contact person
__ Enhancement request system
__ Response time ranges
__ User's forums
__ Scheduled conferences or webinars
__ Training for new releases
__ Implementation schedule and milestones
__ Assessment of district personnel's understanding during implementation
__ Role of the district in the process (e.g., implementation support, resident "experts")

EXHIBIT 8.4
Technology Decision Making: Aligning Personnel Resources
Beyne, S., (2009) Presentation at the California Educational Technology Professionals Association Confer-
ence: Aligning Personnel Resources, San Diego, CA. Reprinted with permission of Digital Schools, LP,
Volo, IL, and Salinas, CA (2012).

A more comprehensive approach to looking for efficiencies and increased productivity is the use of a performance audit. Performance audits can be used to determine how economical each of the school district's operations is and their efficiency. They can also be utilized to identify weaknesses in the system as well as compliance issues. Auditing firms or consultants familiar with the overall operations of school systems and their compliance issues most often execute performance audits.

SUMMARY

The use of technology in managing human resources will continue to grow. In the past, human resource management has been driven by the business side's need to account for personnel and budgets and process payroll. In the future, the opposite will be true. The management of the human resources will drive the business side of education. The idea that human resources is basically a recruiting, employment, and evaluation function has long past. Human resource departments of the future more closely resemble their private counterparts, providing an array of services and functions.

Human resources is the single biggest driver of costs in a school district. They are not only the most important educational resource but are also a school district's biggest asset. Performance, productivity, and efficiency are becoming important drivers of educational and human resources. Ensuring that school districts have the appropriate staff to be effective and, at the same time, efficient has prompted the use of process mapping and personnel/performance audits. Outsourcing and shared services have also become an important component of resource management and personnel where they are allowed by state law. With more and more emphasis on site-based management, all levels of administration now have input into staffing decisions and allocations.

CASE STUDY

Bottom Falls School District is growing rapidly. In 2000, the district was composed of one high school, one middle school, and three elementary schools. Today, the district has two high schools, two middle schools, and six elementary schools. The superintendent and board of education have decided it is now time to hire a full-time human resource director. After careful consideration, they have asked you to assume the position. Your first step is to outline the duties and parameters of the department. The second step is to make recommendations regarding the implementation of a human resources software system.

EXERCISES AND DISCUSSION QUESTIONS

1. In the school system in which you work or reside, how are resource allocation decisions determined? Is there a process for evaluating whether resources result in increased student performance?
2. Utilizing the case study, how would you work with other administrators to ensure that staff is allocated and accounted for appropriately? What features would you look for in a software system for the human resource department?
3. In your professional life, what choices have you made with regard to allocating human resources to improve achievement? How did you determine whether they were successful?
4. What should be the role of the principal, superintendent, and board of education in allocating human resources and evaluating their effectiveness?

5. Using the process mapping technique outlined in the chapter, diagram your school district's hiring process. Review your diagram, and reflect on the process. Are there any ways it could be improved, or are there any redundant steps that could be eliminated to make it more efficient?

6. If faced with the task of having to significantly reduce the expenditures in a school or school district, how would you go about it? How would human resources affect your decision?

7. What are the pros and cons of giving principals control over a school's personnel allocation?

8. Interview the administrator in charge of human resources in your district. Ascertain how well the current human resource software meets the needs of the district. What are the strengths and weaknesses of the software? Does the district utilize a position control system?

REFERENCES

Baroody, K. (2011). Turning around the nation's lowest-performing schools: Five steps districts can take to improve their chances of success. *Center for American Progress.*

Beyne, S., (2009) Presentation at the California Educational Technology Professionals Association Conference: Aligning Personnel Resources, San Diego, CA.

Beyne, S., & Bedford, M. (2009). Business and HR integration through position control: The information technology interface. *DataBus.* Winter, v. 2009 i. 1, pp. 26–27

Beyne, S., & Bedford, M. (2011). Bending the trend: Lowering personnel expenditures for K–12 schools. *California School Business News* May v. 44 n, 8, pp. 3–4.

Brill, S. (2011). *Class warfare: Inside the fight to fix America's schools.* New York: Simon & Schuster.

Bureau of Labor Statistics, U.S. Department of Labor. (2012). *Occupational Outlook Handbook*, 2012–13 edition. http://www.bls.gov/ooh/office-and-administrative-support/home.htm.

Center for Comprehensive School Reform and Improvement. (2009). *Reallocating resources for school improvement—Context for resource allocation.* http://www.centerforcsri.org/pubs/reallocation/context.html.

Cook, D. (1979). *Program evaluation and review technique: Applications in education.* Washington, DC: University Press of America.

Daggett, W. (2009). *Effectiveness and efficiency framework—A guide to focusing resources to increase student performance.* http://www.leadered.com/pdf/EE%20 %20White%20Paper%20website%203.25.09.pdf.

Fox, F., and Prombo, M. (2010). Program cuts. *Illinois Association of School Business Officials Update Magazine, 18* (2), 32–35.

Newstead, B., Saxton, A., & Colby, S. J. (2008). Going for the gold: Secrets of successful schools. *Education Digest, 74* (2), 9–16.

Schilling, C. (2006). General session presented at the Jamaican Association of School Bursars Annual Meeting: Entrepreneurship in Education, Jamaica.

U.S. Census Bureau. U.S. National Center for Education Statistics (2012). *Digest of Education Statistics.*

U.S. Census Bureau. U.S. National Center for Education Statistics (2012). *Projections of Educational Statistics.*

Wong, O., & Casing, D. (2010). *Equalize student achievement: Prioritizing money and power.* Lanham, MD: Rowman & Littlefield Education.

Zirkel, P. A. (2011). State laws and guidelines for RTI: Additional implementation features. *Communiqué.* http://www.nasponline.org/publications/cq/39/7/ professional-practice-state-laws.aspx.

Epilogue

Human resource management is an ever-evolving area of school leadership. This book provides many of the strategies and practices of effective school resource management. There are many challenges facing school leaders, and our ability to manage employees is crucial for school success and student outcomes. The purpose of this epilogue is to summarize key points from the book and provide some of the major educational challenges that must be addressed if we are to be successful in the future.

There are many government laws that are impacting the education of students and educators. No Child Left Behind and Race to the Top are just a couple examples of the federal government influencing state educational goals and consequently how schools teach our children and young adults.

As of fall 2012, thirty-three states had been given waivers from No Child Left Behind. States continue to fail to meet testing targets. In 2011, 48 percent of America's public schools failed to meet No Child Left Behind testing standards. And in California, 66 percent of the public schools had failed to meet the standards. Across the nation, schools continue to struggle to meet state and federal standards, and meeting these standards will become more challenging with less funding. Requests for waivers and alternative testing programs will undoubtedly continue.

As of fall 2012, federal legislators continue to debate educational funding. Arnie Duncan, secretary of education, commented that "services would have to be slashed for more than 1.8 million disadvantaged students, and thousands of teachers and aides would lose jobs when the automatic budget cuts kick in" (Gonzalez, 2012). However Congressman Richard Shelby stated that "our nation cannot continue to spend money we don't have" (Gonzalez, 2012). The U.S. economy continues to struggle, and there is uncertainty among many people, especially regarding unemployment; jobs; a balanced budget; and federal, capital gains, and corporate tax rates. All these factors impact the funding of our education system.

There continues to be a need for better collaboration among federal legislators. Congressman Tom Harkin said that "we all must come together with good will to hammer out a balanced agreement that will not only prevent sequestration, but reduce our deficit and protect America's families" (Gonzalez, 2012). Meanwhile, educators face the challenge of uncertainty and "doing more with less." Undoubtedly, educators need to be creative in managing their fiscal and human resources.

Not only are there resource issues, but administrators are also faced with a myriad of *human resource* and *organizational challenges.* Administrators need to be equipped to recruit talented human resources to meet the educational demands of the school system. Therefore, the primary goal of human resources planning is to forecast the future needs of an organization and to ensure that all resources are obtained, anticipate changes in staffing, understanding and staying current with federal and state laws and local district policies, and working with the school community to match future needs and current organizational resources with future resources. For example, financial constraints and ideology differences are creating tensions between school boards and teacher unions, as demonstrated by the September 2012 Chicago teachers strike. There were many issues involved, such as pay, benefits, class size, school closings, procedures, and teacher evaluation. This has had a major impact on the community and students in this third-largest school district in the nation. The impact of these conflicts impact sentiments toward unions, boards, and charter schools. Besides Chicago, other cities across the nation are facing pressures for school change, such as reductions in art programs at the Denver Public Schools, New Jersey's plan to implement a new statewide teacher evaluation program, California and New York public school program reductions, and teacher recruitment and preparation changes in Kentucky.

Given the progressing financial constraints, *compensation of employees* will continue to be an issue. Compensation represents about 80 percent or more of the school district total budget. Educators and the board will need to carefully examine all the factors that motivate employees for good performance other than only relying upon compensation. They will also need to rely upon other creative compensation structures, such as pay-for-performance, skills-based, knowledge-based, gain-sharing, and merit plans that can be successfully utilized.

Proposing creative and different *compensation structures* will undoubtedly create increased conflict among the board, teachers, and unions, as evidenced by the Lake Forest School District 115, Illinois, proposed salary restructuring. This will demand increased challenges in the collective bargaining process and call for all parties to work collaboratively to reach agreement. The collective bargaining process will need to be approached by all parties with good-faith intentions with the students' education as a foremost goal given the constraints of financial resources.

The *operations of the school* are highly dependent upon adequate safety and security, transportation, custodial care, facility maintenance, and meaningful auxiliary programs. All these programs impact the employees of a school district. Administrators and the board will need to continue to be resilient and creative in managing human resources to meet these needs and ensure all the proper certification is obtained. While major metropolitan and large school districts have sophisticated human resource systems, smaller school systems are just recognizing the importance of such software. Technology will play an even bigger role in human resource planning in the future. Human resources will not only drive school business systems but also include features that will make it easier for administrators to predict and account for current and future staffing needs. This is especially critical as more and more school districts relinquish more control to individual schools and sites. Last, districts are finding creative solutions to addressing noncore functions in their schools, such as outsourcing and sharing services.

In summary, future school leaders will fundamentally need to learn how to *do more with less*. They will need to be skilled in process mapping and organizational improvement strategies to maximize resources, improve current operations, and manage human resources. This approach consists of identifying obstacles (wastes, bottlenecks, redundancies, delays, conflicts, inadequate technology, and budget systems) that hinder efficiency among human resources and overall school management.

Educators will need to employ viable actions (value-added solutions) to address obstacles, provide accountability for fiscal stability, and optimize human resource practices. Last, school leaders will need to assist all stakeholders in understanding the ever-important paradigm of efficient *fiscal stewardship* to maximize the limited resources for the education of students and meet the future demands of our community, government agencies, society, and workforce.

REFERENCE

Gonzalez, A. (2012). *Education secretary urges balanced budget cuts.* Associated Press.

Appendix A
Employee Rights, National Labor Relations Act

Employees covered by the National Labor Relations Act (NLRA) are guaranteed the right to form, join, decertify, or assist a labor organization and to bargain collectively through representatives of their own choosing or to refrain from such activities. Employees may also join together to improve terms and conditions of employment without a union.

Employees covered by the NLRA are afforded certain rights to join together to improve their wages and working conditions, with or without a union.

UNION ACTIVITY

Employees have the right to attempt to form a union where none currently exists or to decertify a union that has lost the support of employees.

Examples of employee rights include:

- Forming, or attempting to form, a union in your workplace;
- Joining a union, whether the union is recognized by your employer or not;
- Assisting a union in organizing your fellow employees;
- Refusing to do any or all of these things; and
- Being fairly represented by a union.

ACTIVITY OUTSIDE A UNION

Employees who are not represented by a union also have rights under the NLRA. Specifically, the National Labor Relations Board (NLRB) protects the rights of employees to engage in "protected concerted activity," which is when two or more employees take action for their mutual aid or protection regarding terms and conditions of employment. A single employee may also engage in protected concerted activity if he or she is acting on the authority of other employees, bringing group complaints to the employer's attention, trying to induce group action, or seeking to prepare for group action.

A few examples of protected concerted activities are:

- Two or more employees addressing their employer about improving their pay;
- Two or more employees discussing work-related issues beyond pay, such as safety concerns, with each other; and
- An employee speaking to an employer on behalf of one or more coworkers about improving workplace conditions.

WHO IS COVERED?

Most employees in the private sector are covered by the NLRA. However, the act specifically excludes individuals who are:

- employed by federal, state, or local government;
- employed as agricultural laborers;
- employed in the domestic service of any person or family in a home;
- employed by a parent or spouse;
- employed as an independent contractor;
- employed as a supervisor (supervisors who have been discriminated against for refusing to violate the NLRA may be covered);
- employed by an employer subject to the Railway Labor Act, such as railroads and airlines; and
- employed by any other person who is not an employer as defined in the NLRA.

Source: https://www.nlrb.gov/rights-we-protect/employee-rights.

Appendix B
Employer/Union Rights and Obligations

The law forbids employers from interfering with employees in the exercise of rights to form, join, or assist a labor organization for collective bargaining or from working together to improve terms and conditions of employment or refraining from any such activity. Similarly, labor organizations may not interfere with employees in the exercise of these rights.

The National Labor Relations Act (NLRA) forbids employers from interfering with, restraining, or coercing employees in the exercise of rights relating to organizing, forming, joining, or assisting a labor organization for collective bargaining purposes or from working together to improve terms and conditions of employment or refraining from any such activity. Similarly, labor organizations may not restrain or coerce employees in the exercise of these rights.

Examples of employer conduct that violates the law:

- Threatening employees with loss of jobs or benefits if they join or vote for a union or engage in protected concerted activity;
- Threatening to close the plant if employees select a union to represent them;
- Questioning employees about their union sympathies or activities in circumstances that tend to interfere with, restrain, or coerce employees in the exercise of their rights under the act;
- Promising benefits to employees to discourage their union support;

- Transferring, laying off, terminating, assigning employees more difficult work tasks, or otherwise punishing employees because they engaged in union or protected concerted activity; and
- Transferring, laying off, terminating, assigning employees more difficult work tasks, or otherwise punishing employees because they filed unfair labor practice charges or participated in an investigation conducted by National Labor Relations Board (NLRB).

Examples of labor organization conduct that violates the law:

- Threats to employees that they will lose their jobs unless they support the union;
- Seeking the suspension, discharge, or other punishment of an employee for not being a union member even if the employee has paid or offered to pay a lawful initiation fee and periodic fees thereafter;
- Refusing to process a grievance because an employee has criticized union officials or because an employee is not a member of the union in states where union security clauses are not permitted;
- Fining employees who have validly resigned from the union for engaging in protected concerted activities following their resignation or for crossing an unlawful picket line;
- Engaging in picket line misconduct, such as threatening, assaulting, or barring nonstrikers from the employer's premises; and
- Striking over issues unrelated to employment terms and conditions or coercively enmeshing neutrals into a labor dispute.

WHAT RULES GOVERN COLLECTIVE BARGAINING FOR A CONTRACT?

After employees choose a union as a bargaining representative, the employer and union are required to meet at reasonable times to bargain in good faith about wages, hours, vacation time, insurance, safety practices, and other mandatory subjects. Some managerial decisions, such as subcontracting, relocation, and other operational changes, may not be mandatory subjects of bargaining, but the employer must bargain about the decisions' effects on unit employees.It is an *unfair labor practice* for either party to refuse to bargain collectively with the other, but parties are not compelled to reach agreement or make concessions.

If after sufficient good faith efforts no agreement can be reached, the employer may declare impasse and then implement the last offer presented to the union. However, the union may disagree that true impasse has been reached and file a charge of an unfair labor practice for failure to bargain in good faith. The NLRB will determine whether true impasse was reached based on the history of negotiations and the understandings of both parties. If the board finds that impasse was not reached, the employer will be asked to return to the bargaining table. In an extreme case, the NLRB may seek a federal court order to force the employer to bargain.

The parties' obligations do not end when the contract expires. They must bargain in good faith for a successor contract or for the termination of the agreement while terms of the expired contract continue. A party wishing to end the contract must notify the other party in writing sixty days before the expiration date or sixty days before the proposed termination. The party must offer to meet and confer with the other party and notify the Federal Mediation and Conciliation Service of the existence of a dispute if no agreement has been reached by that time.

HOW IS "GOOD FAITH" BARGAINING DETERMINED?

There are hundreds, perhaps thousands, of NLRB cases dealing with the issue of the duty to bargain in good faith. In determining whether a party is bargaining in good faith, the board will look at the totality of the circumstances. The duty to bargain in good faith is an obligation to participate actively in the deliberations so as to indicate a present intention to find a basis for agreement. This implies both an open mind and a sincere desire to reach an agreement as well as a sincere effort to reach a common ground.

The additional requirement to bargain in "good faith" was incorporated to ensure that a party did not come to the bargaining table and simply go through the motions. There are objective criteria that the NLRB will review to determine if the parties are honoring their obligation to bargain in good faith, such as whether the party is willing to meet at reasonable times and intervals and whether the party is represented by someone who has the authority to make decisions at the table.

Conduct away from the bargaining table may also be relevant. For instance if an employer were to make a unilateral change in the terms and conditions of employees' employment without bargaining, that would be an indication of bad faith.

Source: https://www.nlrb.gov/rights-we-protect/employerunion-rights-obligations.

Appendix C
Summary of the Major Laws of the Department of Labor

The Department of Labor (DOL) administers and enforces more than 180 federal laws. These mandates and the regulations that implement them cover many workplace activities for about 10 million employers and 125 million workers.

Following is a brief description of many of the DOL's principal statutes most commonly applicable to businesses, job seekers, workers, retirees, contractors, and grantees. This brief summary is intended to acquaint you with the major labor laws and not to offer a detailed exposition. For authoritative information and references to fuller descriptions on these laws, you should consult the statutes and regulations themselves.

"Employment Laws Assistance" (http://www.dol.gov/compliance/laws/main.htm) provides a list of selected U.S. DOL laws and regulations with links to related compliance assistance activities. The DOL compliance assistance website (http://www.dol.gov/compliance) offers complete information on how to comply with federal employment laws. "Rulemaking and Regulations" (http://www.dol.gov/asp/regs/rulemaking.htm) provides brief descriptions of and links to various sources of information on DOL's rulemaking activities and regulations.

WAGES AND HOURS

The Fair Labor Standards Act (FLSA) prescribes standards for wages and overtime pay that affect most private and public employment. The act is administered by the Wage and Hour Division (http://www.dol.gov/whd). It requires employers to pay covered employees who are not otherwise exempt at least the federal minimum wage and overtime pay of one-and-one-half times the regular rate of pay. For nonagricultural operations, it restricts the hours that children under age sixteen can work and forbids the employment of children under age eighteen in certain jobs deemed too dangerous. For agricultural operations, it prohibits the employment of children under age sixteen during school hours and in certain jobs deemed too dangerous.

The Wage and Hour Division also enforces the labor standards provisions of the Immigration and Nationality Act (INA) that apply to aliens authorized to work in the United States under certain nonimmigrant visa programs (H-1B, H-1B1, H-1C, H2A).

WORKPLACE SAFETY AND HEALTH

The Occupational Safety and Health (OSH) Act is administered by the Occupational Safety and Health Administration (OSHA; http://www.osha .gov). Safety and health conditions in most private industries are regulated by OSHA or OSHA-approved state programs, which also cover public-sector employers. Employers covered by the OSH Act must comply with the regulations and the safety and health standards promulgated by OSHA. Employers also have a general duty under the OSH Act to provide their employees with work and a workplace free from recognized, serious hazards. OSHA enforces the act through workplace inspections and investigations. Compliance assistance and other cooperative programs are also available.

WORKERS' COMPENSATION

The Longshore and Harbor Workers' Compensation Act (LHWCA) administered by the Office of Workers' Compensation Programs (OWCP; http://www.dol.gov/owcp) provides for compensation and medical care to certain maritime employees (including a longshore worker or other person in longshore operations and any harbor worker, including a ship repairer, shipbuilder, and shipbreaker) and to qualified dependent survivors of such employees who are disabled or die due to injuries that occur on the navigable waters of the United States or in adjoining areas customarily used in loading, unloading, repairing, or building a vessel.

The Energy Employees Occupational Illness Compensation Program Act (EEOICPA) is a compensation program that provides a lump-sum payment of $150,000 and prospective medical benefits to employees (or certain of their survivors) of the Department of Energy and its contractors and subcontractors as a result of cancer caused by exposure to radiation or certain illnesses caused by exposure to beryllium or silica incurred in the performance of duty, as well as for payment of a lump-sum of $50,000 and prospective medical benefits to individuals (or certain of their survivors) determined by the Department of Justice to be eligible for compensation as uranium workers under section 5 of the Radiation Exposure Compensation Act (RECA).

The Federal Employees' Compensation Act (FECA), 5 U.S.C. 8101 et seq., establishes a comprehensive and exclusive workers' compensation program that pays compensation for the disability or death of a federal employee resulting from personal injury sustained while in the performance of duty. FECA, administered by OWCP, provides benefits for wage loss compensation for total or partial disability, schedule awards for permanent loss or loss of use of specified members of the body, related medical costs, and vocational rehabilitation.

The Black Lung Benefits Act (BLBA) provides monthly cash payments and medical benefits to coal miners totally disabled from pneumoconiosis (black lung disease) arising from their employment in the nation's coal mines. The statute also provides monthly benefits to a deceased miner's survivors if the miner's death was due to black lung disease.

EMPLOYEE BENEFIT SECURITY

The Employee Retirement Income Security Act (ERISA) regulates employers who offer pension or welfare benefit plans for their employees. Title I of ERISA is administered by the Employee Benefits Security Administration (EBSA; http://www.dol.gov/ebsa; formerly the Pension and Welfare Benefits Administration) and imposes a wide range of fiduciary, disclosure, and reporting requirements on fiduciaries of pension and welfare benefit plans and on others having dealings with these plans. These provisions preempt many similar state laws. Under Title IV, certain employers and plan administrators must fund an insurance system to protect certain kinds of retirement benefits, with premiums paid to the federal government's Pension Benefit Guaranty

Corporation (PBGC; http://www.pbgc.gov). EBSA also administers reporting requirements for continuation of health-care provisions, required under the Comprehensive Omnibus Budget Reconciliation Act (COBRA) of 1985 and the health-care portability requirements on group plans under the Health Insurance Portability and Accountability Act (HIPAA).

UNIONS AND THEIR MEMBERS

The Labor-Management Reporting and Disclosure Act (LMRDA) of 1959 (also known as the Landrum-Griffin Act) deals with the relationship between a union and its members. It protects union funds and promotes union democracy by requiring labor organizations to file annual financial reports; by requiring union officials, employers, and labor consultants to file reports regarding certain labor relations practices; and by establishing standards for the election of union officers. The act is administered by the Office of Labor-Management Standards (OLMS).

EMPLOYEE PROTECTION

Most labor and public safety laws and many environmental laws mandate whistleblower protections for employees who complain about violations of the law by their employers. Remedies can include job reinstatement and payment of back wages. OSHA enforces the whistleblower protections in most laws.

UNIFORMED SERVICES EMPLOYMENT AND REEMPLOYMENT RIGHTS ACT

Certain persons who serve in the armed forces have a right to reemployment with the employer they were with when they entered service. This includes those called up from the reserves or National Guard. These rights are administered by the Veterans' Employment and Training Service (VETS; http://www.dol.gov/vets).

EMPLOYEE POLYGRAPH PROTECTION ACT

This law bars most employers from using lie detectors on employees but permits polygraph tests only in limited circumstances. It is administered by the Wage and Hour Division.

GARNISHMENT OF WAGES

Garnishment of employee wages by employers is regulated under the Consumer Credit Protection Act (CCPA), which is administered by the Wage and Hour Division.

THE FAMILY AND MEDICAL LEAVE ACT

Administered by the Wage and Hour Division, the Family and Medical Leave Act (FMLA) requires employers of fifty or more employees to give up to twelve weeks of unpaid, job-protected leave to eligible employees for the birth or adoption of a child or for the serious illness of the employee or a spouse, child, or parent.

VETERANS' PREFERENCE

Veterans and other eligible persons have special employment rights with the federal government. They are provided preference in initial hiring and protection in reductions in force. Claims of violation of these rights are investigated by VETS.

GOVERNMENT CONTRACTS, GRANTS, OR FINANCIAL AID

Recipients of government contracts, grants, or financial aid are subject to wage, hour, benefits, and safety and health standards under:

- The Davis-Bacon Act, which requires payment of prevailing wages and benefits to employees of contractors engaged in federal government construction projects;
- The McNamara-O'Hara Service Contract Act, which sets wage rates and other labor standards for employees of contractors furnishing services to the federal government; and
- The Walsh-Healey Public Contracts Act, which requires payment of minimum wages and other labor standards by contractors providing materials and supplies to the federal government.
- Administration and enforcement of these laws are by the Wage and Hour Division. The Office of Federal Contract Compliance Programs (OFCCP; http://www.dol.gov/ofccp) administers and enforces three federal contract-based civil rights laws that require most federal contractors and subcontractors,

as well as federally assisted construction contractors, to provide equal employment opportunity. The Office of the Assistant Secretary for Administration and Management's (OASAM; http://www.dol.gov/oasam) Civil Rights Center administers and enforces several federal assistance based civil rights laws requiring recipients of federal financial assistance from DOL to provide equal opportunity.

MIGRANT AND SEASONAL AGRICULTURAL WORKERS

The Migrant and Seasonal Agricultural Worker Protection Act (MSPA) regulates the hiring and employment activities of agricultural employers, farm labor contractors, and associations using migrant and seasonal agricultural workers. The act prescribes wage protections, housing, and transportation safety standards; farm labor contractor registration requirements; and disclosure requirements. The Wage and Hour Division administers this law.

FLSA exempts agricultural workers from overtime premium pay but requires the payment of the minimum wage to workers employed on larger farms (farms employing more than approximately seven full-time workers). The act has special child-labor regulations that apply to agricultural employment; children under sixteen are forbidden to work during school hours and in certain jobs deemed too dangerous. Children employed on their families' farms are exempt from these regulations. The Wage and Hour Division administers this law. OSHA also has special safety and health standards that may apply to agricultural operations.

INA requires employers who want to use foreign temporary workers on H-2A visas to get a labor certificate from the Employment and Training Administration (http://www.doleta.gov) certifying that there are not sufficient, able, willing, and qualified U.S. workers available to do the work. The labor standards protections of the H-2A program are enforced by the Wage and Hour Division.

MINE SAFETY AND HEALTH

The Federal Mine Safety and Health Act of 1977 (Mine Act) covers all people who work on mine property. The Mine Safety and Health Administration (MSHA; http://www.msha.gov) administers this act. The Mine Act holds mine operators responsible for the safety and health of miners, provides for the setting of mandatory safety and health standards, mandates miners' training requirements, prescribes penalties for violations, and enables inspectors to close dangerous mines. The safety and health standards address numerous hazards including roof falls, flammable and explosive gases, fire, electricity, equipment rollovers and maintenance, airborne contaminants, noise, and respirable dust. MSHA enforces safety and health requirements at more than 13,000 mines, investigates mine accidents, and offers mine operators training and technical and compliance assistance.

CONSTRUCTION

Several agencies administer programs related solely to the construction industry. OSHA has special occupational safety and health standards for construction; the Wage and Hour Division, under Davis-Bacon and related acts, requires payment of prevailing wages and benefits; OFCCP enforces Executive Order 11246, which requires federal construction contractors and subcontractors, as well as federally assisted construction contractors, to provide equal employment opportunity; the anti-kickback section of the Copeland Act precludes a federal contractor from inducing any employee to sacrifice any part of the compensation required.

TRANSPORTATION

Most laws with labor provisions regulating the transportation industry are administered by agencies outside the DOL. However, longshoring and maritime industry safety and health standards are issued and enforced by OSHA. The LHWCA requires employers to assure that workers' compensation is funded and available to eligible employees. In addition, the rights of employees in the mass transit industry are protected when federal funds are used to acquire, improve, or operate a transit system. Under the federal transit law, the DOL is responsible for approving employee protection arrangements before the Department of Transportation can release funds to grantees.

PLANT CLOSINGS AND LAYOFFS

Such occurrences may be subject to the Worker Adjustment and Retraining Notification Act (WARN). WARN offers employees early warning of impending layoffs or plant closings. The Employment and Training Administration (ETA; http://www.doleta.gov) provides information to the public on WARN, though neither ETA nor the DOL has administrative responsibility for the statute, which is enforced through private action in the federal courts.

ADVISORIES

For more details and guidance on laws and regulations covered in this fact sheet, call the appropriate DOL agency listed in your phone book under "U.S. Government." Other federal agencies besides the DOL enforce laws and regulations that affect employers.

Statutes that ensure nondiscrimination in employment are generally enforced by the Equal Employment Opportunity Commission (EEOC, http://www.eeoc.gov). The Taft-Hartley Act regulates a wide range of employer-employee conduct and is administered by the National Labor Relations Board (NLRB; http://www.nlrb.gov). For more information on these laws, consult these agencies; they are listed in your phone book under "U.S. Government."

Source: http://www.dol.gov/opa/aboutdol/lawsprog.htm.

Appendix D
Laws Enforced by the Equal Employment Opportunity Commission

TITLE VII OF THE CIVIL RIGHTS ACT OF 1964 (TITLE VII)

This law (http://www.eeoc.gov/laws/statutes/titlevii.cfm) makes it illegal to discriminate against someone on the basis of race, color, religion, national origin, or sex. The law also makes it illegal to retaliate against a person because the person complained about discrimination, filed a charge of discrimination, or participated in an employment discrimination investigation or lawsuit. The law also requires that employers reasonably accommodate applicants' and employees' sincerely held religious practices unless doing so would impose an undue hardship on the operation of the employer's business.

THE PREGNANCY DISCRIMINATION ACT

This law (http://www.eeoc.gov/laws/statutes/pregnancy.cfm) amended Title VII to make it illegal to discriminate against a woman because of pregnancy, childbirth, or a medical condition related to pregnancy or childbirth. The law also makes it illegal to retaliate against a person because the person complained about discrimination, filed a charge of discrimination, or participated in an employment discrimination investigation or lawsuit.

THE EQUAL PAY ACT (EPA) OF 1963

This law (http://www.eeoc.gov/laws/statutes/epa.cfm) makes it illegal to pay different wages to men and women if they perform equal work in the same workplace. The law also makes it illegal to retaliate against a person because the person complained about discrimination, filed a charge of discrimination, or participated in an employment discrimination investigation or lawsuit.

THE AGE DISCRIMINATION IN EMPLOYMENT ACT (ADEA) OF 1967

This law (http://www.eeoc.gov/laws/statutes/adea.cfm) protects people who are forty or older from discrimination because of age. The law also makes it illegal to retaliate against a person because the person complained about discrimination, filed a charge of discrimination, or participated in an employment discrimination investigation or lawsuit.

TITLE I OF THE AMERICANS WITH DISABILITIES ACT (ADA) OF 1990

This law (http://www.eeoc.gov/laws/statutes/ada.cfm) makes it illegal to discriminate against a qualified person with a disability in the private sector and in state and local governments. The law also makes it illegal to retaliate against a person because the person complained about discrimination, filed a charge of discrimination, or participated in an employment discrimination investigation or lawsuit. The law also requires that employers reasonably accommodate the known physical or mental limitations of an otherwise qualified individual with a disability who is an applicant or employee unless doing so would impose an undue hardship on the operation of the employer's business.

SECTIONS 102 AND 103 OF THE CIVIL RIGHTS ACT OF 1991

Among other things, this law (http://www.eeoc.gov/laws/statutes/cra-1991. cfm) amends Title VII and the ADA to permit jury trials and compensatory and punitive damage awards in intentional discrimination cases.

SECTIONS 501 AND 505 OF THE REHABILITATION ACT OF 1973

This law (http://www.eeoc.gov/laws/statutes/rehab.cfm) makes it illegal to discriminate against a qualified person with a disability in the federal government. The law also makes it illegal to retaliate against a person because the person complained about discrimination, filed a charge of discrimination, or participated in an employment discrimination investigation or lawsuit. The law also requires that employers reasonably accommodate the known physical or mental limitations of an otherwise qualified individual with a disability who is an applicant or employee unless doing so would impose an undue hardship on the operation of the employer's business.

THE GENETIC INFORMATION NONDISCRIMINATION ACT (GINA) OF 2008

Effective November 21, 2009, this law (http://www.eeoc.gov/laws/statutes/gina.cfm) makes it illegal to discriminate against employees or applicants because of genetic information. Genetic information includes information about an individual's genetic tests and the genetic tests of an individual's family members, as well as information about any disease, disorder, or condition of an individual's family members (i.e., an individual's family medical history). The law also makes it illegal to retaliate against a person because the person complained about discrimination, filed a charge of discrimination, or participated in an employment discrimination investigation or lawsuit.

Source: Equal Employment Opportunity Commission (http://www.eeoc.gov/laws/statutes/index.cfm).

Appendix E
Prohibited Employment Policies/Practices

Under the laws enforced by the Equal Employment Opportunity Commission (EEOC), it is illegal to discriminate against someone (applicant or employee) because of that person's race, color, religion, sex (including pregnancy), national origin, age (forty or older), disability, or genetic information. It is also illegal to retaliate against a person because he or she complained about discrimination, filed a charge of discrimination, or participated in an employment discrimination investigation or lawsuit. The law forbids discrimination in every aspect of employment.

The laws enforced by EEOC prohibit an employer or other covered entity from using neutral employment policies and practices that have a disproportionately negative effect on applicants or employees of a particular race, color, religion, sex (including pregnancy), or national origin or on an individual with a disability or class of individuals with disabilities if the polices or practices at issue are not job related and necessary to the operation of the business. The laws enforced by EEOC also prohibit an employer from using neutral employment policies and practices that have a disproportionately negative impact on applicants or employees age forty or older if the policies or practices at issue are not based on a reasonable factor other than age.

JOB ADVERTISEMENTS
It is illegal for an employer to publish a job advertisement that shows a preference for or discourages someone from applying for a job because of his or her

race, color, religion, sex (including pregnancy), national origin, age (forty or older), disability, or genetic information. For example, a help-wanted ad that seeks "females" or "recent college graduates" may discourage men and people over forty from applying and may violate the law.

RECRUITMENT

It is also illegal for an employer to recruit new employees in a way that discriminates against them because of their race, color, religion, sex (including pregnancy), national origin, age (forty or older), disability, or genetic information. For example, an employer's reliance on word-of-mouth recruitment by its mostly Hispanic workforce may violate the law if the result is that almost all new hires are Hispanic.

APPLICATION AND HIRING

It is illegal for an employer to discriminate against a job applicant because of his or her race, color, religion, sex (including pregnancy), national origin, age (forty or older), disability, or genetic information. For example, an employer may not refuse to give employment applications to people of a certain race.

An employer may not base hiring decisions on stereotypes and assumptions about a person's race, color, religion, sex (including pregnancy), national origin, age (forty or older), disability, or genetic information.

If an employer requires job applicants to take a test, the test must be necessary and related to the job, and the employer may not exclude people of a particular race, color, religion, sex (including pregnancy), national origin, or individuals with disabilities. In addition, the employer may not use a test that excludes applicants age forty or older if the test is not based on a reasonable factor other than age.

If a job applicant with a disability needs an accommodation (such as a sign language interpreter) to apply for a job, the employer is required to provide the accommodation, so long as the accommodation does not cause the employer significant difficulty or expense.

JOB REFERRALS

It is illegal for an employer, employment agency, or union to take into account a person's race, color, religion, sex (including pregnancy), national origin, age (forty or older), disability, or genetic information when making decisions about job referrals.

JOB ASSIGNMENTS AND PROMOTIONS

It is illegal for an employer to make decisions about job assignments and promotions based on an employee's race, color, religion, sex (including pregnancy), national origin, age (forty or older), disability, or genetic information. For example, an employer may not give preference to employees of a certain race when making shift assignments and may not segregate employees of a particular national origin from other employees or from customers.

An employer may not base assignment and promotion decisions on stereotypes and assumptions about a person's race, color, religion, sex (including pregnancy), national origin, age (forty or older), disability, or genetic information.

If an employer requires employees to take a test before making decisions about assignments or promotions, the test may not exclude people of a particular race, color, religion, sex (including pregnancy), or national origin or individuals with disabilities unless the employer can show that the test is necessary and related to the job. In addition, the employer may not use a test that excludes employees age forty or older if the test is not based on a reasonable factor other than age.

PAY AND BENEFITS

It is illegal for an employer to discriminate against an employee in the payment of wages or employee benefits on the bases of race, color, religion, sex (including pregnancy), national origin, age (forty or older), disability, or genetic information. Employee benefits include sick and vacation leave, insurance, access to overtime as well as overtime pay, and retirement programs. For example, an employer many not pay Hispanic workers less than African-American workers because of their national origin, and men and women in the same workplace must be given equal pay for equal work.

In some situations, an employer may be allowed to reduce some employee benefits for older workers but only if the cost of providing the reduced benefits is the same as the cost of providing benefits to younger workers.

DISCIPLINE AND DISCHARGE

An employer may not take into account a person's race, color, religion, sex (including pregnancy), national origin, age (forty or older), disability, or genetic information when making decisions about discipline or discharge. For example, if two employees commit a similar offense, an employer many not discipline them differently because of their race, color, religion, sex (including pregnancy), national origin, age (forty or older), disability, or genetic information.

When deciding which employees will be laid off, an employer may not choose the oldest workers because of their age. Employers also may not discriminate when deciding which workers to recall after a layoff.

EMPLOYMENT REFERENCES

It is illegal for an employer to give a negative or false employment reference (or refuse to give a reference) because of a person's race, color, religion, sex (including pregnancy), national origin, age (forty or older), disability, or genetic information.

REASONABLE ACCOMMODATION AND DISABILITY

The law requires that an employer provide reasonable accommodation to an employee or job applicant with a disability unless doing so would cause significant difficulty or expense for the employer.

A reasonable accommodation is any change in the workplace (or in the ways things are usually done) to help a person with a disability apply for a job, perform the duties of a job, or enjoy the benefits and privileges of employment.

Reasonable accommodation might include, for example, providing a ramp for a wheelchair user or providing a reader or interpreter for a blind or deaf employee or applicant.

REASONABLE ACCOMMODATION AND RELIGION

The law requires an employer to reasonably accommodate an employee's religious beliefs or practices unless doing so would cause difficulty or expense for the employer. This means an employer may have to make reasonable adjustments at work that will allow the employee to practice his or her religion, such as allowing an employee to voluntarily swap shifts with a coworker so that he or she can attend religious services.

TRAINING AND APPRENTICESHIP PROGRAMS

It is illegal for a training or apprenticeship program to discriminate on the bases of race, color, religion, sex (including pregnancy), national origin, age (forty or older), disability, or genetic information. For example, an employer may not deny training opportunities to African-American employees because of their race. In some situations, an employer may be allowed to set age limits for participation in an apprenticeship program.

HARASSMENT

It is illegal to harass an employee because of race, color, religion, sex (including pregnancy), national origin, age (forty or older), disability or genetic information. It is also illegal to harass someone because they have complained about discrimination, filed a charge of discrimination, or participated in an employment discrimination investigation or lawsuit.

Harassment can take the form of slurs, graffiti, offensive or derogatory comments, or other verbal or physical conduct. Sexual harassment (including unwelcome sexual advances, requests for sexual favors, and other conduct of a sexual nature) is also unlawful. Although the law does not prohibit simple teasing, offhand comments, or isolated incidents that are not very serious, harassment is illegal if it is so frequent or severe that it creates a hostile or offensive work environment or if it results in an adverse employment decision (such as the victim being fired or demoted). The harasser can be the victim's supervisor, a supervisor in another area, a coworker, or someone who is not an employee of the employer, such as a client or customer. Harassment outside of the workplace may also be illegal if there is a link with the workplace; for example, if a supervisor harasses an employee while driving the employee to a meeting.

TERMS AND CONDITIONS OF EMPLOYMENT

The law makes it illegal for an employer to make any employment decision because of a person's race, color, religion, sex (including pregnancy), national origin, age (forty or older), disability, or genetic information. That means an employer may not discriminate when it comes to such things as hiring, firing, promotions, and pay. It also means an employer may not discriminate, for example, when granting breaks, approving leave, assigning work stations, or setting any other term or condition of employment—however small.

PRE-EMPLOYMENT INQUIRIES (GENERAL)

As a general rule, the information obtained and requested through the pre-employment process should be limited to those essential for determining if a person is qualified for the job, whereas information regarding race, sex, national origin, age, and religion are irrelevant in such determinations. Employers are explicitly prohibited from making pre-employment inquiries about disability.

Although state and federal equal opportunity laws do not clearly forbid employers from making pre-employment inquiries that relate to or disproportionately screen out members based on race, color, sex, national origin, religion, or age, such inquiries may be used as evidence of an employer's intent to discriminate unless the questions asked can be justified by some business purpose. Therefore, inquiries about organizations, clubs, societies, and lodges of which an applicant may be a member or any other questions that may indicate the applicant's race, sex, national origin, disability status, age, religion, color, or ancestry if answered should generally be avoided. Similarly, employers should not ask for a photograph of an applicant. If needed for identification purposes, a photograph may be obtained after an offer of employment is made and accepted.

Prohibited Pre-Employment Inquiries and Questions:

- Race
- Height and weight
- Credit rating or economic status
- Religious affiliation or beliefs
- Citizenship
- Marital status, number of children
- Gender
- Arrest and conviction
- Security/background checks for certain religious or ethnic groups
- Disability
- Medical questions and examinations

DRESS CODE

In general, an employer may establish a dress code that applies to all employees or employees within certain job categories. However, there are a few possible exceptions. While an employer may require all workers to follow a uniform dress code even if the dress code conflicts with some workers' ethnic beliefs or practices, a dress code must not treat some employees less favorably because of their national origin. For example, a dress code that prohibits certain kinds of ethnic dress, such as traditional African or East Indian attire, but otherwise permits casual dress would treat some employees less favorably because of their national origin. Moreover, if the dress code conflicts with an employee's religious practices and the employee requests an accommodation, the employer must modify the dress code or permit an exception to the dress code unless doing so would result in undue hardship. Similarly, if an employee requests an accommodation to the dress code because of his disability, the employer must modify the dress code or permit an exception to the dress code unless doing so would result in undue hardship.

CONSTRUCTIVE DISCHARGE/FORCED TO RESIGN

Discriminatory practices under the laws EEOC enforces also include constructive discharge or forcing an employee to resign by making the work environment so intolerable a reasonable person would not be able to stay.

Source: EEOC, http://www.eeoc.gov/laws/practices/index.cfm.

Index

About the Authors

Daniel R. Tomal is a professor of educational leadership at Concordia University Chicago, River Forest, Illinois. He has been a public high school teacher, administrator, corporate vice president, and professor. He received his B.S. and M.A.E. degrees in education from Ball State University and a Ph.D. in educational administration and supervision from Bowling Green State University. He has consulted numerous schools and has testified before the U.S. congress. While a professor at Purdue University North Central, he was voted "Outstanding Teacher." Dan has authored ten books and over one hundred articles and research studies. He has made guest appearances on numerous radio and television shows, such as CBS's *This Morning*, NBC's *Cover to Cover, Les Brown, Joan Rivers, Tom Snyder,* CBN's *700 Club,* ABC's *News,* and *WYLL Chicago Talks.* He is author of the books *Action Research for Educators,* a CHOICE Outstanding Academic Title, *Resource Management for School Administrators* (with Craig Schilling), and *Challenging Students to Learn.*

Craig A. Schilling is an associate professor of educational leadership at Concordia University Chicago, River Forest, Illinois. He has been a public school administrator, systems analyst, and CEO. He received his B.S. degree in sociology from the University of Maryland; M.S. in human services from Boston University; and Ed.D. in educational administration from Northern Illinois

University. He has consulted numerous school districts and has spoken and presented at over one hundred workshops and training seminars throughout the United States, Canada, and the Caribbean. He has served as an expert witness in school finance cases. Craig has served as the president of the Illinois Association of School Business Officials (IASBO), on the board of directors of the Association of School Business Officials International, and on the Illinois Financial Accounting Committee. In 1999, the Association of School Business Officials awarded him an Eagle Service Award for contributions to the profession of school business management. He is coauthor of *Resource Management for School Administrators* (with Daniel Tomal).